Exploring Worship ANEW

Dreams and Visions

Pamela Ann Moeller

Chalice Press
St. Louis, Missouri

All scripture quotations, unless otherwise indicated, are from the *New Revised Standard Version Bible,* copyright 1989, Division of Christian Education of the National Council of the Churches of Christ in the USA. Used by permission.

Cover design: Judy Newell
Art direction: Elizabeth Wright
Interior design: Elizabeth Wright

This book is printed on acid-free, recycled paper.

Visit Chalice Press on the World Wide Web at
www.chalicepress.com

10 9 8 7 6 5 4 3 2 1   98 99 00 01 02 03

Library of Congress Cataloging–in–Publication Date

(Pending)

Printed in the United States of America

Exploring
Worship
ANEW

Table of Contents

Part V. Building Worship Events from the Ground Up

Part VI. Coming Full Circle

Preface

This volume finds its roots in personal experience in a wide variety of worship contexts in diverse places, most of them relatively safe on the one hand, and on the other, fertile ground for struggle and challenge. Raised a Lutheran, ordained a Presbyterian (USA), I have studied and worshiped at ecumenical, Presbyterian, Roman Catholic, and Methodist institutions. I have taught and worshiped at a Lutheran seminary and in a theological college of the United Church of Canada. Geographically speaking, I have been shaped in part by Manhattan and commuter Long Island, New York, by rural and urban Illinois, Indiana, Georgia, and Saskatchewan, by metro Toronto and small-town Ontario, along with any number of diverse locations within the confines of North America.

The essence of the content within has withstood the fire of the classroom and the challenge of the sanctuary over many years. The visions and designs I describe are grounded in actual practice at the colleges where I have taught and engaged in significant ways in the colleges' worship life and among congregations where I have worshiped and served as worship consultant, designer, preacher, presider. Those who have worked with me I acknowledge here: students in my classroom, pastors who have extended invitations to preach and then engaged in preliminary scene-setting, and members of congregations who have given precious time and energy to work together toward creating a worship event for their community. Without them this volume would have never come to be. Most especially I am grateful to students—far too many to name—who year after year asked me when I would publish my lectures so they could have them in hand. At long last, their wish, which has sustained me in moments when I have been inclined to give up, is coming true.

I am thankful, too, for those who have taught me, or at least tried. Among them, John Burkhart, Don Wardlaw, Don Saliers, and Fred Craddock—as teachers, mentors, colleagues, and friends—deserve special mention. So does Joan Wyatt, pastor of Trinity St. Paul's United Church, who has staunchly supported my work, along with the congregation, who graciously received my offerings and whose members and staff worked with me, making chapter 15 a possibility.

It has been a delight to work with my editor, Jon L. Berquist. He has encouraged me with his strong affirmations and assisted me with his thoughtful suggestions. The final word, though, belongs to the Source of all, and so, *Soli Deo Gratia*.

Acknowledgments

Chapter 2: Naming Reality: Reflections on the Waters of Baptism. The core of this chapter was published in *The Canadian Liturgical Society Newsletter* 4/3 (Fall 1994).

Chapter 5: Embodied Preaching. This chapter is drawn largely from my book *A Kinesthetic Homiletic: Embodying Gospel in Preaching* (Minneapolis: Fortress Press, 1993).

Chapter 6: Time and the "Christian Year." This essay appeared in an earlier form in the *Newsletter of the Canadian Liturgical Society* 4/3 (1994).

Chapter 9: Just Language. This chapter is a revision of an earlier essay, "The Language of the Gospel," published in *Consensus* 18/1 (1992).

Chapter 13: The Integrality of Worship. This chapter in its original form appeared in the *Papers of the Academy of Homiletics* (1992).

Chapter 14: Collaborators in Creation. Much of the content of this chapter appeared as "Creating Worship Events," *Worship* 69/1 (January 1995).

Chapter 15: Sampler. This appeared in an earlier form in the *Papers of the Academy of Homiletics* (1995).

Introduction

The church has always raised questions about worship. We can see those questions between the lines of scripture and in the composing of the early extracanonical documents like the *Didache* and Justin's *Apology*. Questions about worship shaped the various Reformations in significant ways as individuals and whole communities developed their own visions and patterns of worship. More recently, questions of worship have been set alight by the work of Vatican II, by vigorous research into the history of worship, and by a real restlessness in denominations whose membership has been leaching or flooding away.

Two new patterns have risen to dominance as a result of contemporary questions about and experiences of church and worship: the "convergence liturgy" approach to worship and the "seeker-sensitive" approach to worship. The former is rooted in ecumenism and the felt need to develop a common worship pattern that will enable Christians to experience unity in Christ despite denominational differences and to witness that unity in the world. The "convergence" form and content, particularly with regard to sacramental praxis, are rooted in the presumed third century composite text known as the *Apostolic Tradition of Hippolytus*,[1] and both traditional and contemporary versions of this scheme are evident in all the denominational books of worship recently published.[2]

---

[1] Paul Bradshaw discusses briefly the problems of authenticity regarding this document, and suggests "…one ought not automatically to assume that it provides reliable information about the life and liturgical activity of the church in Rome in the early third century." Paul F. Bradshaw, *The Search for the Origins of Christian Worship: Sources & Methods for the Study of Early Liturgy* (New York: Oxford University Press, 1992), 89–92.

[2] Two of the best volumes available to those who want to look more deeply into the "convergence" approach are: Don E. Saliers, *Worship as Theology: Foretaste of Glory Divine* (Nashville: Abingdon Press, 1994), and Gordon W. Lathrop, *Holy Things: A Liturgical Theology* (Minneapolis: Fortress Press, 1993).

The "seeker-sensitive" approach shows impatience with the traditionalism of the "convergence" pattern, finding it irrelevant to contemporary reality. "Seeker-sensitive" worship aims to attract the unchurched by using the aspects and resources of modern society such as the sounds and techniques of popular music, motivational speaking, and the like.[3] The so-called megachurches offer the most dramatic examples of this approach.

It is easy to get caught up in deconstruction or defense of these approaches and participate in a new manifestation of the worship wars that have long haunted the worship life within congregations and between denominations. In point of fact, either pattern has the potential of being relevant or irrelevant, faithful or unfaithful. Yet at a time when the church is, in the view of many, in a precarious place when many in even a nominally Christian society question its credibility and value—let alone in a multifaith world where science, technology, and multinational corporate policy seem to be creating the world in their image—we cannot afford the luxury of worship wars. We need vibrant, life-giving worship that will build community, paint in vivid colors the economy, the *kin*dom of God, that will empower us in new ways to work as God's bodies in building a world grounded in and constructed with love.

Purpose

The purpose of this book, then, is to try and lay a different kind of groundwork for thinking about and doing worship. Through an integration of experience, research, constructive theology, and plain old intuition and imagination, I want to invite readers into new experiences of worship. I aim to release the theological and practical imagination of all kinds of Christians toward developing a worship praxis (an ongoing circle of reflection, action, reflection, action) that is attentive to both the riches of Christian tradition and the gifts and struggles of an always changing complex of realities. I hope that together we can increasingly create worship that is profoundly gospel—good news: loving, just, organic, life-giving not just for ourselves, but for the entire cosmos. For me as well as for my readers, that likely means pushing beyond the horizon of what is comfortable and safe, beyond the limits and hindrances of this book, beyond

---

[3]The best discussion of this issue can be found in Daniel Benedict and Craig Kennet Miller, *Contemporary Worship for the 21st Century: Worship* or *Evangelism?* (Nashville: Discipleship Resources, 1994). The volume includes a useful bibliography. A more recent response to the seeker approach from a conservative Lutheran perspective is Marva J. Dawn, *Reaching Out without Dumbing Down: A Theology of Worship for the Turn-of-the-Century Culture* (Grand Rapids: Eerdmans, 1995).

orthodoxy. This is risky business, but as many of our global sisters and brothers know, being Christian *is* risky.

Character

Like some of the fourth century church leaders who seem to have thought one ought to experience baptism before talking about it, and unlike those who advise preachers to "tell 'em what you are going to say, say it, and then tell 'em what you said," I will not describe here what is to come. I will say that this work does not pretend to address every issue or implication or to develop a systematic theology of worship or worship theology, but rather to offer touchstones, images, possibilities. If you expect a series of chapters that are mirror images of each other, albeit treating various aspects of what constitutes worship, you may be pleasantly surprised. Committed as I am to diversity of worship styles, I have endeavored to maintain some diversity of approaches to writing about worship!

Additionally, if, in spite of my disclaimer above, you still expect a wholesale critique or endorsement of either "convergence" or "seeker-sensitive" approaches, you may be relieved. If you want to have at the end of your reading a sure and certain road map that will guarantee you successful worship (whatever you think that is), I can only hope you are open to a different kind of journey. In aid of this, you may find it helpful to muse a while on each chapter—or at least each part—before going on, long enough, at least, to allow your own dreams and visions to begin to develop and move you to a new place in the mystery of worshiping.

Fundaments

I believe that there are many wonderful and faithful ways of engaging in worship and that there cannot be a normative pattern for worship that is good for all times and places. Nor do I believe there is a magic process for developing worship events, although I do have strong commitments in this regard as the following chapters will reveal. I maintain particular theological biases as well. You will find these interwoven through the chapters that follow, but I will spell them out in brief here as a quick reference point for those who find such helpful.

1. **Gospel is the event of God engaging in ongoing love for and with us** by inviting and empowering us to live in loving, dialogical relationship with God and all creation. The life, death, resurrection of Christ, and the ongoing life of the Spirit uniquely manifest this gospel that "belongs" to all people.

2. **We worship by living in loving, dialogical relationship with God and all creation. Worship** *events* **are concentrated, microcosmic experiences of that macrocosm of relationality.**

3. **As gospel belongs to all people, so worship and worship events do likewise, start to finish.** Thus all people related to a congregation have gifts to offer and need to be actively involved in planning, implementing, and assessing worship events.

4. **God relates with us as whole persons in our particularity,** in the here and now, in all our diverse physical, emotional, intellectual, spiritual, sexual, personal, and corporate dimensions and contexts. Thus what we do in worship events needs to attend to our dynamic, present, whole-bodied reality. **Worship events are thus intrinsically contextual**—we cannot assume what has "worked" elsewhere or else-when is appropriate here and now.

5. Everything in a worship event manifests a theological praxis. **The theological core of a worship event is the Spirit empowered gospel experience of particular text(s) of the day in relationship with the particular community of faith.**

6. **Gospel and, therefore, worship events, are innately linked with the entirety of our lives in the world;** we cannot separate Sunday morning from the rest of our being and doing. Whenever we gather for worship, we do so in direct relation to politics, arts, economy, ecology, technology—and all other facets of life in an almost-twenty-first-century global community. Thus **worship events are not only for our own good, but,** as Alexander Schmemann has said, **"for the life of the world."**[4]

At the bottom of all this, readers may see the "great commandment" to love God and one's neighbor as oneself, evidenced particularly but not only in scripture's portrayals of Jesus' life.[5] If, as the Reformers so fundamentally believed, worship is to be grounded biblically, it cannot for me be located anywhere else than in loving, dialogical relationality. Although

---

[4]Alexander Schmemann, *For the Life of the World: Sacraments and Orthodoxy* (Crestwood, New York: St. Vladimir's Seminary Press, 1973).

[5]Indeed, Augustine of Hippo thought that scripture was fundamentally addressed toward love of God and love of neighbor. Augustine, "On Christian Doctrine," *A Select Library of the Nicene and Post-Nicene Fathers of the Christian Church*, Vol. 2. Philip Schaff, ed. (Edinburgh: T. & T. Clark/Grand Rapids: Eerdmans, 1890/1993, I (36) 40), 533. Philo's concept of eucharistia as eucharistic *life* strengthens the organic wholeness of my perspective, as does Calvin's understanding and practice of worship along with his insistence on the global dimensions of Christian life.

not unchallenged in scripture, this vision provides for me the bottom line of the essential biblical witness in a world where such love seems to me to be entirely too rare. Beyond this, scripture simply does not give us a comprehensive or prescriptive address of worship.[6]

Love God, love neighbor, love self—and not in that order, but inseparably. We simply cannot do one without the other—it is all or nothing. If there is anything simple or normative about worship for me, this is it. "Well and good," I can hear my friend and colleague Don Wardlaw say, "but what does it look like walking around?"[7] Worship as living in loving, dialogical relationship with God and neighbor needs to be fleshed out, explored in depth, expressed dynamically on Sunday morning. Then it needs to be reflected on again. What follows begins that. The rest—whether it be a different departure or a further development—is left to you.

Perhaps it will help, as I suggested above, if you stop and muse at the end of each chapter. Ask yourself what theological claims I make and whether or not they resonate in any way with your own theology and practice or offer something new. If you were to pursue something of what I suggest, put a theological perspective into practice, or even push beyond my proposal, what might the implications be for your ministry, your community? Even if nothing here seems to apply to you and your context, perhaps this volume will offer an opportunity to reflect anew on your own theology and practice and, ultimately, to explore the question of how what we think and do in regard to worship shapes our lives.

Finally, because worship belongs to all people, I invite you to consider how you can involve others in your faith community in this work—perhaps reading and musing together in worship event or study group. After all, God blesses all people with divine love, grants each gifts for worship, and creates everyone with the potential to be the agent of the Spirit in the shaping of new, worshipful living. If this volume can enhance this dialogical relationship of worship in even a small way, it will be worth every moment of the years of work that have gone into its coming into being.

---

[6]Even if it did, such content would needfully come under all the scrutiny and provisos we continually address to all the rest of the Bible, and its implications for contemporary worship would require constant reassessment.

[7]This was Don's pointed and persistent question to me when I took his "Growth in Preaching Course" almost two decades ago.

PART I

Setting the Scene

CHAPTER 1

The Necessity and Nature
of Worship

The hand of God came upon me, and brought me out by the spirit and set me down in the middle of a valley; it was full of bones. God led me all around them; there were very many lying in the valley, and they were very dry. God said to me, "Mortal, can these bones live?" I answered, "O God, you know." Then God said to me, "Prophesy to these bones, and say to them, O dry bones, hear the word of God. Thus says God to these bones: I will cause breath to enter you, and you shall live. I will lay sinews on you, and will cause flesh to come upon you, and cover you with skin, and put breath in you, and you shall live; and you shall know that I am God. So I prophesied as I had been commanded; and as I prophesied, suddenly there was a noise, a rattling, and the bones came together, bone to its bone. I looked, and there were sinews on them, and flesh had come upon them, and skin had covered them; but there was no breath in them. Then God said to me, "Prophesy to the breath, prophesy, mortal, and say to the breath: Thus says God, come from the four winds, O breath, breathe upon these slain, that they may live." I prophesied as God commanded me, and the breath came into them, and they lived, and stood on their feet, a vast multitude.

(Ezekiel 37:1–10, NRSV, adapted)

The Human Condition: Dying for Want of Gospel

It had been the worst year of his life. His last job was a disaster—he and his colleagues simply inhabited different planets. After months of fighting off their demands that he compromise his principles, he finally was let go. He wound up trekking across the entire continent to find another position, piling the trauma of a move onto the trauma of job-change. That also meant leaving behind life-sustaining relationships—and absence rarely makes the heart grow fonder, just more lonely. But he moved and started everything over. He felt utterly uprooted, disconnected, alien. His new colleagues were pleasant, but they were clearly settled quite comfortably in their ruts and foxholes. Other than sticking their heads up once in a while like Wiarton Willy or Punxatawny Phil, they were remarkably disinterested in him. Meanwhile, the thought of bars and singles groups shivered his timbers head to toe.

As for the churches in town, well, he visited lots of them, most more than once. He struggled his way through bulletins, prayer books, hymnbooks, saying and singing words that seemed to have little, if anything, to do with him, his life, his world. He watched choirs process and liturgical dancers dance; he watched baptisms and confirmations and commissionings. He heard sermons about untrustworthy politicians and exorbitant bank profits; sermons about what is wrong with people today, in terms of age or sex or ethnicity, and declining membership in the church. He heard sermons about the importance of remodeling the church, and about how difficult it is to be a Christian, and about "family values." What he didn't hear and didn't experience beyond a shadow of a doubt was gospel: that he was loved, that he mattered to somebody, that he belonged.

Yes, he was handed a bulletin, and sometimes somebody put a crumb of bread in his hand and allowed a sip of wine to slip between his lips. But the eyes around him studiously refused to hold his and it, finally, was obvious that Christ's table or no, he really wasn't welcome, he really didn't belong. When September rolled around again and the prospect of another year of feeling like he must be a leper stared him squarely in the face, he went home one night, put a pistol in his mouth, and pulled the trigger.

This story is a composite of several peoples' stories. It may have been the story behind the first funeral I did—of a man who *did* end his life in this way. It is not the kind of story with which one wants to begin a book, let alone one's ministry. But it and others like it, including holocaust stories of whole groups of people—Jews, women, the poor—have been more than enough to convince me that people are dying for want of gospel.

People *are* dying for want of being fed not just bread crumbs and a drop of moisture, but the rich milk of loving kindness that makes it clear they are welcome no matter what. People are dying for lack of knowing that they, in all their uniqueness and tediousness, truly belong, that they don't just exist, but *matter*—and not only because of their function, but because they *are*. Day by day people die senseless deaths only because no one has caught them up in the embrace of relationship with God in which one experiences oneself (consciously or not) as an honest-to-God member of God's family. People die for want of good news which will enable them to live perhaps for the first time, to become whom they are meant to be: members of God's beloved family of friends participating in the feast of life if only proleptically and partially, but nonetheless really, joyfully, and richly.

Humanity has provisioned our world with people dying for want of gospel. Some die violently and horrifyingly, like those wherever war currently rages. Others disintegrate away like an old, much-fingered road atlas or dictionary. Some starve to death in East Africa or die of neglect, forgotten in some corner of the city of Toronto or Toledo. For many, everything may seem to be fine until the sudden death of their child or the discovery they have lupus. Perhaps others feel a vague sense of unease or maybe even outright rebellion, but these, our sisters and brothers, are dying nonetheless.

We can blame this tragic reality on the snake in the Garden of Eden if we want. We can blame malice or simple human fallibility or greed or fear of "the other." But wherever we place the blame, for me the bottom line remains the same: like the dry bones in Ezekiel's valley, we may exist, but without deep, loving relationship with both the Source of life and other participants in creation, we have not one breath of Life.

Who God Is: Lover, Life-giver

Ezekiel, among others, envisioned with extraordinary clarity *not* a God who weighs us, finds us wanting, throws up the divine hands in utter disgust, and abandons us for some people in some other galaxy who have got their heads on straight. On the contrary, Ezekiel recognized Eternal Compassion, who seeks us out for the very purpose of raising up our dead bones, clothing us with muscles and infusing us with holy spirit so that we truly live. Sharing the same vision, John Calvin speaks of God as the One who, seeing our desperate state, out of incredible, nonstop love, seeks us out again and again through every kind of vehicle—the law, the prophets, Jesus of Nazareth, gospel, the spirit, the church, water, food, drink, theologians, teachers, pastors, neighbors, the homeless, the refugee. Calvin says God "never tires in repeatedly...heaping new gifts upon us."[1] God loves us profoundly and intimately.

---

[1]John Calvin, *Institutes of the Christian Religion* ed. John T. McNeill, tr. F. L. Battles (from the 1559 Latin text edited by Barth and Neisel, [*Joannis Calvini Opera Selecta* vols. 3, 4,5] including collations from earlier editions of that text and versions of the Institutes), (Philadelphia: Westminster Press, 1960), 2.7.7.

God's love gives us life, sustains it, redeems it over and over again, and enriches life beyond our imaginations. God loves us lavishly, never fails us, and always finds new modes of expressing that love to us.[2] Suffusing us with love, God breathes life into us again and again with the same regularity and persistence of the daily bath and three square meals with which we may be blessed. It is just this that Christ Jesus is about, and the gospel Christ bodied forth: that God embraces all people as beloved friends no matter our wretchedness; that God is home for us, claiming humankind as family, so we need never be alone or hungry for love, so we need never succumb to absolute despair. People who met Jesus experienced this steadfast, open love: the leper, the Samaritan woman, the centurion with the sick servant, the thief on the cross, the bent-over woman, Lazarus, and finally even intellectually challenged Peter, as well as rigid-as-a-brick Saul/Paul. This is love that just doesn't stop: flesh-and-blood-walking-about affirmation of the worth of the absolutely worthless for all the world to see.

Worship Events: A Matter of Death—or Life?

When we talk about worship we are talking about the bones and the beings in Ezekiel's valley and about a matter of death or life. I do not believe that worship can kill. But I know from experience that events called worship can petrify our hearts, minds, and bodies. They can run roughshod over us with languages that trivialize, exclude, negate, or violate us; they can lock us up in personal piety closets, drain us of hope, or send us scrambling madly to get out into a world that seems to be more real, make more sense, and offer a better chance at sanity and survival. Experiences that do this are precisely *not* worship. Yet, how many of us have not suffered this near-death masqueraded as Sunday morning worship?

Worship events have to do with death, no doubt. They must recognize its reality, name it in its multifaceted forms, and respect its power. After all, we all come to death ourselves, and few of us would deny that a healthy life journey—any life journey—cannot proceed without many encounters with death. So life and death do not really describe a duality, polar opposites, but an organic whole. In my view life embraces death, contains it. What else could resurrection mean? And yet, not only did "Good" Friday happen, we see endless repetitions of it in the brutal murders of innocent infants, in the bloody assaults upon women and seniors, in gay-bashing and eruptions of racial hatred, in people dying for no

---

[2]*Institutes,* 3.20.36, and Pamela Ann Moeller, *Calvin's Doxology: Worship in the 1559 Institutes with a View to Contemporary Worship Renewal* (Allison Park, Pa.: Pickwick Publications, 1997), 27.

reason at all except lack of love. Here we know death in the extreme, a malevolent horror entirely too prevalent in our lives.

Worship Events: God's Gift of Life

For precisely this reason, we—and our entire cosmos—need worship events to generate life. Christians are not "Good" Friday people but Easter people, resurrection people, people who major in life. Most important, we are Easter people not because *we* breathed on that early Sunday morning, but because *God* breathed life into *us*, *breathes* life into us day in and day out. So worship events are, as Calvin knew, particular, concentrated moments when, first and foremost, God breathes life into, names, feeds, teaches, comforts, and, yes, even challenges, God's beloved ones. In these moments God invites us to participate in a choreography that God always begins with "I love you."

It doesn't matter whether we have come to anoint the dead, are cowering behind closed doors, or are planning to preach the sermon that will ultimately catapult us to greatness. God nevertheless begins with "I love you" and provides us with opportunity for concentrated, concrete, and clearly identifiable experiences of being caught up in lavish, loving relationship with God and with neighbor.

These experiences, worship events, can be imagined as living water that keeps us afloat, and clean inside and out, and able to see clearly through the muddiness of daily living or as the staff of life and vigorous drink that nourish and warm us, and provide us with the strength and energy, to be what and who we are supposed to be. We have every reason to hope that worship events will incarnate the Word that names our world and ourselves and embraces us into the unshakeable conviction that we are loved; that there will be the kiss of peace which binds us to our neighbors and makes them part of us,[3] so that we could no more neglect them or do them harm than we could neglect to brush our teeth or fill our stomachs. We need worship events to be the glue that keeps us together body and soul when life tumbles in like row upon row of dominoes sometimes for years at a time, but even more we ought to be able to trust that they will catch us up in the vision and promise that inspire us to be truly human and to do for the world what we could never do otherwise.

Ultimately, occasions of worship aim to root us in life itself, with the One who is life itself, without whom we are little more than excruciatingly painful figments of our own imaginations. Worship occasions thus function as formative phenomena. They shape us as persons with individual

---

[3]Matthew 5:23–24.

identities, ideas, and behavior, precisely as gospel comes addressed to us by name—as our baptisms affirm—as the food and fluid, sound and sight, speech and act that move across and through my body *ipso facto* become intensely, intimately mine.

Events-in-Community

Nonetheless, worship transcends the personal and individual. These events of substance, sound, silence, movement, affect and effects are events-*in-community*. We cannot be in loving, caring relationship with God without being in the same kind of relationship with the human community around the sanctuary. Witness the great commandment that unqualifiedly says to love God *and* neighbor. Yes. Observe Jesus manifesting God's love to all kinds of people, and most especially, to those deemed most *unlov-able*. Note the suggestion that those of us who are alienated from other human beings would do well to leave our gift for God at the door and go repair the broken relationship. Observe the fact that everything that happens on Sunday morning is done by, for, and with other human beings. Some preach, others hear; we hand things into others' hands; one does not baptize oneself, but is touched by water and by human fingers with members of the community of God, at the very least, looking on. If we sing or dance a solo, we do so because God has given us the gift, and because others listen and watch. In the exchange of peace we come eye to eye and body to body with those created in the image of God, in whom we may see the face of Christ and the working of the Spirit. Through others we experience the Divine, and through us, the Holy One bodies forth. Nothing happens in isolation; even the inmost secret prayers of the heart the whole people set before God.

We do not function as individual computers beeping happily away on our own pet programs. We participate in a worldwide web—linked by live current and multidirectional lines of communication and a (sometimes all-too-invisible) matrix of love. We cannot be connected with God and unplugged from our neighbors in the pew: God's gift of love to us engages us in and commissions us to multidimensional living, because we *are* dependent upon one another not only for our smooth running, but for our very being. Worship events, as embodiments of Eternal Compassion, fundamentally connect with what it means to be human: relating with the cosmos through eating, drinking, moving, thinking, through touch, sound, movement, word, smell, sight. In such experiences we are meant to discover who we are, that we belong, that we are profoundly and unfailingly loved. In worship events we are meant to learn ways and means of living, living connectedly, living lovingly.

Holistic Worship

We can no longer think, then, of worship as a private experience, or even as an aggregate but fundamentally independent experience. Nor can we think of it as primarily cerebral or spiritual, but disembodied. God relates with us holistically. We process sermons,[4] we do theology, worship, live with nerves, gastric juices, DNA and RNA, backs, thighs, and elbows, hand to hand, body to body with our neighbors in the pew. Such a claim may shock us, depending on our cultural sensitivities and given Christianity's long history of denigrating the body. Yet our body, our being, our worship life are radically relational, holistically relational. Almost all of scripture tells us this, the theological premise of incarnation tells us this. And what else does it mean to say we belong to the *body* of Christ, the family of God?

More, we are woven together with creation in the same way that nerve, muscle, blood, and bone cells were woven together in our mother's womb. We are braided together with the cosmos by the very air that wafts through canyons, washes over mountains and prairies, and that we breathe; by the water that constitutes us and covers huge portions of the earth. The very star-stuff that grounds us all intimately connects us with the whole cosmos.

Worship times, spaces, gatherings may serve in part and for a time as sanctuary from the pain and struggle of life rooted in the complex matrix of flesh/spirit/self/other. But worship rooted in the God of Life seeks not to keep separate but to make whole. So, welcoming strangers into the intimacy of our room in God's house, sharing together the most important words and acts of life, we can come to know that the gaunt, haunted AIDS victim in Brasilia, as well as in Springfield or Winnipeg, and the unnamed, malnutritioned, about-to-die infant in Sri Lanka or New South Wales are children of our genetic line and our blood siblings. Splashed with the healing waters of God's love for us, we become partners in the healing of the planet's ecosystems. Receiving with relief the gifts of loaf and cup, we can come to know that the political party in power as well as the opposition need, as much as you and I, constant, absurdly generous experiences of God's love. Embraced by an exchange of peace or swept up in the mystery of a much-loved hymn exactly when we do not recognize ourselves or when we feel most lost, we can come to discover our responsibility for the care of endangered species. We cannot be closet Christians.

---

[4]Thomas H. Troeger, "Emerging New Standards in the Evaluation of Effective Preaching," *Worship* 64/4 (1990), 294.

Into worship events we also bring our life experiences and those of our global community and stitch them together in intentional, focused engagement with loving God and with each and every other. The argument in the car on the way to church is the sin that is forgiven; last night's TV news story on world hunger reveals new dimensions to the gift of loaf and cup. Cleaning up the ruins left by the latest flood or choking in the smoke of burning forests reconfigures our bath in the waters of baptism.

Worship events do not separate us from the unhappy vicissitudes of life, but engage us in primary experience of what it means to be fully human, what it means to live in loving, dialogical relationship with God and God's extended family. Having had life breathed into us during the worship event, we, like Ezekiel and the women at the tomb, discover how to embody that breath of life into the rest of the world.

For the Sake of the Cosmos

Worship events can *never* be an end in themselves, or our quintessential response to/praise of God. Our true response to God and thus our ultimate praise and thanks to God is our whole life in graced relationship with our entire world and all its inhabitants. Worship events thus bring us life—and engage us in life for the life of the world.

What we do in worship events shapes the world. Everything that happens in such an event embodies a particular theology *to* the world, because what occurs in our worship events forms our ideas and our behavior for the rest of our week and the rest of our life, and through us either enhances life in the world or strengthens the power of death over creation. The world is dying for want of Good News, for want of the love of God, for want of knowing itself loved, fed, healed—no matter how polluted and corrupted and irresponsible it is. And we are responsible, because we are the eyes, hands, hearts, bodies of God in the world.

We can never know for sure who will join the gathering of a Sunday morning, but we will always know that everyone will be in need of profound, lavish experiences of love—as will everyone we and they encounter. So ensuring that our worship gatherings are properly ordered, and that we perform the right gesture at the rite moment, and that there is enough food and drink to go around will never be sufficient. What matters is that our worship coheres with gospel, that it "offers Christ," that it breathes life, that it connects most profoundly the lavish love of God with all that we are as human beings. Over and over again a worship event needs to provide opportunity to experience concretely and unquestionably loving relationship with God and neighbor.

We are not talking of tokens here, of a faint taste of love to come, but of the full-bodied nourishment of a hearty meal providing as much as we can eat. We are speaking of the potent and heady pizzazz of deep relationship, tingling all our nerve endings and inspiriting us with Pentecost exhilaration, leading us to storefront or political front to work toward bringing all human hungers to an end. We are embodying love which is bountiful beyond our imaginations and is never, never used up. We are shouting, dancing, 1 Corinthians 13[5] all over again, not just in one thing but in everything, not just read out as the epistle or even preached from the pulpit, but lived out in the way your eyes meet mine in the passing of peace and the gentle touch of your hand as you place a bulletin or cup in my own.

Worship as Life

Worship is thus *our whole life*—our breath, our food, our work, our play. It encompasses human *being:* birth to funeral, night and day, inhale, exhale, rise and fall, black, white, and all the shades of the rainbow, solitude and multinational conversation. Worship is our reality as Christians, the whole out of which and in which we come to know who we are, who God is, and who we are in relation with God and other. Worship constitutes the stuff of Christian life, shaping and shaped by every relationship and every experience, in the laboratory, grocery store, and office, on the ice-skating rink or subway, at the family reunion or street party. Worship is what it means to be human, to be connected with God and all humanity through our shared experiences of hunger and thirst, laughter and weeping; it is being for God by being for all creation just as God is unequivocally for us. Worship events are microcosmic experiences of that economy, the place, time, experience where God and humankind most purposefully meet. No small matter this!

---

[5]"If I speak in the tongues of mortals and of angels, but do not have love, I am a noisy gong or a clanging cymbal. And if I have prophetic powers, and understand all mysteries and all knowledge, and if I have all faith, so as to remove mountains, but do not have love, I am nothing. If I give away all my possessions, and if I hand over my body so that I may boast, but do not have love, I gain nothing. Love is patient; love is kind; love is not envious or boastful or arrogant or rude. It does not insist on its own way; it is not irritable or resentful; it does not rejoice in wrongdoing, but rejoices in the truth. It bears all things, believes all things, hopes all things, endures all things. Love never ends…faith, hope, and love abide, these three; and the greatest of these is love" (1 Corinthians 13:1–8a, 13, NRSV).

Essentials of Life
with God and
Neighbor

CHAPTER 2

Naming Reality: Reflections on the Waters of Baptism

I was baptized on December 21, 1947, when I was less than a month old. I do not, of course, remember the event consciously. That doesn't matter. As was true for Martin Luther, what does matter is *that* I am baptized. It seems I have always known this, quite apart from having been taught the formal theories about baptism and certainly apart from my "confirmation," a catechesis and ritual that have always been empty of positive value for me.

The truth is, I have trouble with common theologies of baptism.[1] I am uncomfortable, as well, with some of the scriptural metaphors for baptism that seem to shape these theologies. Not the least of these are the related notions of baptism as cleansing from original sin, rebirth, and initiation into the church. No matter how I look at this constellation of ideas, it seems plainly to suggest that my mother, who risked her life with me,[2] didn't do the job right. Nor her mother, nor her mother's mother. Moreover, baptism described this way says God doesn't love us as we come into being, DNA strand by DNA strand knit together in the womb, surrounded by the most precious water of all. It flies in the face of the goodness of God as creator, parent, companion. Baptism of this sort suggests we have to be fixed to be acceptable; something has to be done to

---

[1] Readers may find useful John H. McKenna's assessment of how baptism went astray around theologies of original sin and how that might be corrected. John H. McKenna, "Infant Baptism: Theological Reflections," *Worship* 70/1 (May 1996).

[2] According to the *Toronto Star,* June 12, 1996, UNICEF's annual Progress of Nations report, released the prior day, revealed the shocking information that *over a half million women* die yearly from pregnancy and childbirth. The report also indicates that "for every woman who dies, another 30 suffer permanent injury, infection, and disability."

qualify us to participate in God's unmeritable love, in life with God. This God doesn't seem so loving, after all. My own baptism tells me something quite different and infinitely more precious. The poet Isaiah mentors me here, both in vision and in poetic genre.

> But Zion said, "YHWH has forsaken me; my God has forgotten me." Can a woman forget the baby at her breast? Can she fail to cherish the child of her womb? Yet, even if these forget, I will never forget you. See, I have branded you on the palms of my hand…(Isaiah 49:14–16a, NRSV, adapted).

Baptismal Birthing

It began with mild cramps. After a while her water broke and she thought about how water had sustained her baby's life all these months. She paced back and forth until the cramps became contractions. She erupted in a cold sweat. Shaking with chill, and tension, she curled up in a ball on the floor to ease her back. She breathed deeply, rhythmically, to keep the oxygen flowing, to ease the pain. Sometimes she cried out in anguish, and after a while, the palms of her hands began to bleed where her fingernails dug in.

It was not an easy labor. Time stood still while pain rolled through her like the endless waves of the sea. Once she found herself wondering whose crazy idea this was in the first place. Surely there must be an easier way to give birth to new life than out of one's own self. Soaked, now, with sweat, face streaked with tears, she prayed and panted and pushed. She gasped and moaned, writhed and rolled from side to side; she prayed and panted and pushed. And the child was born.

Gently she freed its nose and mouth of blood and amniotic fluid so it could breathe and yell with utmost freedom. She laid it against her breast and together they rested. Nine months she had carried it within her, nurturing its development with her own body, protecting it with her very life. It would be many more months before this child could even begin to take responsibility for itself, years, perhaps forever. But never mind. She would be there for it, helping it overcome all obstacles and face all dangers; she would be there for it, helping it play and learn and grow— she would be there for it, no matter what. This child was of her body, her amniotic fluid, her blood, sweat, tears. It had left its mark on the palms of her hands and changed forever the passions of her heart.

Can a woman forget the baby at her breast? Can she fail to cherish the child of her womb? Yet, even if these forget, I will never forget you.

Birth as Baptism

The water of baptism is the water of birth, the amniotic fluids of the womb of God. It is the water of tears, the sweat of God's arduous, painful labor of giving birth to us. This water is the blood in the palms of God's hands where the nails carve out our names. It proclaims us born of God— God's own beloved children—before anyone knows if we will ever walk or talk or grow up, and quite apart from how we turn out—responsible or irresponsible, faithful or faithless, thankful or thankless.

The water of baptism proclaims us born of God precisely in being born of Laura, Juanita, Miriam, or Soo Mi. Every human birth brings forth God's own beloved children, children worth an infinity of divine blood, sweat, tears; children worth God's dying for, no matter what. The water of baptism names *what is already true*, rehearses after the fact that all life and every life is gift, birthed of God, God embodied for us by valiant women who surrender their bodies, their selves—never to be the same again—so that we might breathe, run, work, laugh, make love, paint, weep, build our own families or not, as we choose.

The water of baptism shows us what is already true for us by name, and by us, for all people everywhere, whether or not they ever hear the name of Jesus, whether or not they ever know they are God's beloved. We baptize no one; the Eastern formula paints the clearer picture: "you are baptized." We are baptized by our mothers and God together in amniotic fluid; we are baptized by God who then calls us to a font full of water— in some times and places a font shaped as a pregnant woman—to name and enact what is so for everyone ever born and to remind us again and again to live as God's beloved with all people everywhere, for they, too, are God's beloved, "Christian" or no.

Not everyone is baptized as I was, who at the grand old age of twenty-seven days had done little more than eat, sleep, and peep. Because baptism as an older person with a much deeper and wider history was not my gift, I cannot speak of that pattern with the authenticity of one who first came to the font at the age of 12, 37, or 62.[3] But for decades now I have

---

[3] I have not given birth, either, but the many mothers in my classroom affirm my imaginative construction of this phenomenon. Indeed, their faces and their words make it abundantly clear I have dipped deeply into their many experiences.

repeatedly claimed my baptism, immensely grateful for Luther's insight that we are baptized once with water and may daily embrace anew the gift of God's impossible love for us, the reality to which the bath pointed, that which it embodied. In my baptismal history, rooted deep in the memory cells of my brain (cells that remember the words, the feel of the water, the touch of hands even if I cannot summon up those particulars), lies the capacity to recover lost balance, heal new woundedness, and discover new possibilities for living lovingly even in, perhaps especially in, the face of evil.

How I delight, though, in the public spectacle, the wonderful, wild event of another's engagement at the font. Here, whether it be the baptism of infant or elder, I see again the vision in which I was immersed, am immersed still: the vision, promise, and reality of wholeness.

Waters of Healing

Stripped, beaten, left to die in the merciless sun. The dirt of the alley and the salt of his sweat gathered in the gashes and cuts and scratches found the way into his nose and mouth. It was hard to know which agony was worse: the fire in his wounds, the fire in his mouth and throat, or the fire in his broken heart at the inhumanity of his kin.

It wasn't long before the flies found him. Half dead, he couldn't move. But his brain still worked, registering all the torment and the sound of feet passing by, leaving him alone in his agony. No, not alone. Through a red haze of pain he heard steps come close, stop. Go away, he screamed voicelessly. Can't you see I'm almost dead? I have nothing left to be stolen; nothing left to be damaged. You might do me the kindness of a swift kick in the head to end my agony.

But it was not to be. He felt not a kick, but gentle hands turning his nose and mouth out of the dirt. A cool, damp cloth soothed his ravaged face, drops of cool water quenched the fire in his mouth. In time, all his wounds were washed free of blood, dirt, and salt, his bruises and swellings were soaked away, the conflagration in his heart was put out by the cool water of tender, loving care. He lived again—when he thought he was dead; he was washed, soothed, healed, rehydrated—alive. How could he ever forget the one who saved his life? How could he ever take

his life for granted again, or anyone else's—or death, or suffering—or water…?

Healing Water

The water of baptism proclaims us soothed by God, all our fevers
quenched in cool fountains, our wounds rinsed clean of corruption, our
parched mouths and throats refreshed by divine rehydration. Far more
than the morning shower that wakens many of us to a new day, baptismal
waters name us enlivened again by God, our thirsting, dying souls re-
stored to life by living water. This water reveals our lives to be of infinite
value even when all our resources are gone (even if we never had any), no
matter what anyone else thinks. It shows us worthy of all God's love and
care, no matter how we got into the fix we are in, even if it was our own
fault, no matter how bad our situation is. *Baptizatus sum*—I am baptized—
said Martin Luther, when Christendom branded him scum of the earth:
heretic. *Baptizatus sum,* said Martin Luther, because it is not, in the end,
the church that baptizes us, but God (as Augustine knew)—God who
proclaims us loved and wanted even when we would rather die, when
others seek our death, robbers or righteous, whichever they may be.
Baptizata sum—I am baptized! Who, understanding that, could ever take
life for granted again, theirs or anyone else's? How could one fail to see
the worth in all God's family of friends, no matter how they look, or
think, or behave; no matter what they might have done or might do next?

I am baptized, healed, reconciled with all whom I have offended,
who have offended me. Not *because* I am baptized, or because "they" are,
not because I am baptized and "they" are not. It is because God is the
loving source of life, because Holy Wisdom seeks wholeness for all creation. So God's face shines in every face, Christ's hands work in everyone's
hands, life-giving Spirit persists in everyone's daily breath.

Baptism does not do that, but God. Baptism reveals to us what is
already so: that all people, no matter how disintegrated, and the entire
cosmos, no matter how dissembled, are loved by God and thus are our
sisters, brothers, blood kin. Baptism also embodies what is not yet—the
healing of a creation now in crisis, in desperate need of being loved to
life—loving, dialogical, relational life.

Recently, a young Muslim told me that Christians do not believe
Christianity is universal, that Christ came for everyone. Muhammad, he
told me, *did* come for all and Islam *is* universal. I see the young man's
point, even though I disagree with him. But that he thinks of Christians
and Christianity in this way proclaims to me volumes of frightening data

within a Christianity that has limited the true family of God (body of Christ) to those who are initiated into its special corporation. Just this notion has allowed the hideous persecution of Muslims and Jews, for example. Yet if God is the source of life, if Jesus was as socially radical as the biblical witness portrays, how could we limit God's beloved family or the extent and equality of God's love? I am not willing to admit that the Parent of all creatures loves some of us more than others and relates with only some of us as members of the holy household. Even Paul claimed there is neither Jew nor Greek in Christ. But I will not stop there, for it is not only in Christ this is so for me, but in the wholeness of the Holy One. And it is so not only as a future, but as a history from Genesis and all the creation stories of the world right through to the present and into infinity.

Impartial Waters

They didn't get it right away. It took a while to figure it out. They thought at first that they were an exclusive group, a closed community. They thought that because of what had happened, they were special—not just special, really, but unique; not just unique, really, but better than everybody else. They'd been chosen, by God! They'd been led out of captivity, whisked off the road to death and oblivion, given the keys to the economy, the very household of God. You can bet your sweet life they weren't going to let just anyone in.

They got furious as women said "we were there, too—we belong to this!" But they had to admit that it was true. They got hysterical when Ananias wrote and said he had let that murderous Saul in. But when they had calmed down and let Barnabas tell the rest of the story about what Saul/Paul was doing, they had to admit that maybe Ananias had done the right thing.

Peter was the last straw. Gentiles, for crying out loud. Common, unclean Gentiles! At least Saul had been a proper, kosher Jew! But Gentiles, for crying out loud. Folks who don't behave properly, who don't think right, who don't speak the same language, who can't possibly understand, who don't deserve this!

Radical Belonging

They didn't get it right away. It took them a while to figure it out. They wandered in the wilderness for a while. They had to learn as they went along. And it took a long time to learn, and even then, it seems they never really caught on. Neither do we. Well, the waters of baptism do not make us perfect, they do not even make us good. They proclaim that God is good. They also reveal that God, in and with each person's individual parents, is everyone's birth parent, the source of everyone's life.

Baptismal waters body forth God's pouring of divine love out for everyone in ever-flowing streams. They show that God is the source of comfort, healing, strength for all. They announce that human lives are of infinite value, no matter what others may think. The waters of baptism reflect the reality that all life comes from God,[4] that all people are born of God, and all are Christ's brothers and sisters; that God loves everybody, even when they aren't "good," especially when they aren't "good," whether or not they are baptized with the church's baptism.

The waters of baptism prophesy, forth-tell, show that in God all have life, life freely given, no matter what we think. They proclaim that because all people are born of God, because all people are beloved of God, we are freed and called to love one another. Who would not share the waters of life with one's brother? Who would not ensure one's sister doesn't die for want of water, water to refresh the parched mouth, water to quench fever, water to wash the corruption from wounds, water to soothe bruises and swellings, water to rehydrate evaporated cells, water to restore to life? Water. *Baptizata sum.* Born of God, the Mother of all mothers. Beloved of God. By the world-full. How, then, could we not love all others as ourselves, baptized or no?

Who deserves this profound, life-giving love? Not the twenty-seven-day-old infant not yet capable of knowing right from wrong; not the faithful "initiate" who has studied and worked ever-so-hard to become a good "church member"; not the sweet soul whose life has been a godsend to everyone he met; nor the irascible, impossible-to-satisfy curmudgeon making everyone's life miserable—not any of these. All of these. Because deserving isn't what matters. Joining the church isn't what matters. What we think isn't what matters. No, we are baptized because God loves us, because we are born of God, because from womb to tomb and beyond God knows us, identifies with us, claims us, loves us. Baptism tells us that. But it doesn't make it so. God makes it so.

Baptism embodies that reality for us Christians, but in regard to all creation. So for me there can be no notion of initiation—by birth *we*

---

[4] "Our God becomes incarnate in every human birth," verse 4, "Tomorrow Christ is Coming," Fredrik Herman Kaan, *Voices United: The Hymn and Worship Book of the United Church of Canada* (Toronto: The United Church Publishing House, 1996), no. 27.

already belong, and we belong to the most *inclusive* community of all—the family of God.There can be no special rites of admission, no partial membership, no exclusive privileges, and no excommunication.There is only the joy of being loved and the ongoing work of loving others as Mother-Father God has loved us and loves us still.

This is the baptism that most powerfully claims me and gives me life: a baptism that names and embodies the reality that *already* is—that God loves and is intimately present with humankind and each individual before any one of us comes to awareness, that God loves us in the messiness and pain of birth, in the newness of birth, in the wretchedness, misery, evil that comes to us or that we create for ourselves, that God loves us into relationship with one another and all others. The creation stories, the psalms, the prophets, the life/death/resurrection of Jesus, the continuing presence of love (no matter how little) in the church, in the world all tell me this. Holy love for us abounds, as the waters of the oceans, the waters of the womb, the enormous percentage of the body that is water, water shared with the thirsty. Shall a woman forget the baby at her breast? Even should she, yet never will I forget you.

Keeping Our Hearts Open

No doubt others will find different baptismal metaphors, biblical or not, to be life-giving. Indeed, those presented in scripture seem to be more individual interpretations of personal experience than any coherent theological view or even a well-stitched quilt of views. So we, too, need to ask about people's experiences—of water, with which we began the chapter—and of relationship.

My own experience and that of many others has demonstrated over and over again how often women, children, the poor, the non-Christian have been suppressed and even crucified by the church in the name of Christ. For that reason, metaphors of "putting on Christ" and "dying and rising with Christ," for example, that are commonly exalted in baptismal liturgies, strike terror in my heart. Perhaps they along with the rebirth image are appropriate for some, but we need to consider carefully whether these images endorse death more than life for anyone. Whether or not they do, congregations and denominations need to enhance accessibility to the *diversity* of possibilities and engage in conversation and reflection on which of them seem most faithful in light of both tradition and the immediate context in which God engages us anew. On each occasion of baptism, then, the possibilities need to be considered carefully so that the most appropriate focus can be chosen for that particular event. Over time, we can lift up many images and metaphors of baptism, thereby celebrating the extraordinary character of the love of the Divine for us.

We need also to consider *how* we embody our chosen focal metaphor. Baptism is not about words, after all. Too often baptisms have been hidden from the congregation by family standing between font and congregation. I have been present at many where words flooded the room but water could neither be seen nor heard, and the way the words were said they might as well have been taped. But imagine a different scene: the family and others gathered behind the font or the congregation gathered round; a large, clear pitcher from which a member of the community pours water visibly and vigorously; generous but gentle applications of water and never mind the mess—water *is* messy; a thick bath towel with which to thoroughly dry off, or perhaps, even wrap around the baptized; words that are spare enough that the act with water retains the focus, words that enhance the event and don't just talk about it; words and actions fully shared among all the participants as full partners in manifesting what God does through us.

There are many right ways to do this. In fact, the way we do baptism might well change often, from culture to culture and occasion to occasion, as we integrate what is most gospel-faithful for each person-in-community, for each community in its particular contextual reality. Perhaps, given the devastating pollution of the waters of the earth or conditions of severe drought in a particular location, we will find lavish use of water inappropriate because it models a profligacy that can no longer be sustained. Alternately, abundant use may be precisely what we need in those circumstances, because abundant life-giving water embodies the extravagant love of the Source of Life for us even when we have rendered life-giving water unfit to drink, and because it shows us where we need to go next in our water-relations.

Such decisions will be ours—in community—time and time again; they cannot be made once for all. Our world changes too fast, our realities shift and transform with the speed of light. And, of course, we will make mistakes—there are no guarantees of "success"—whatever that is. We can confidently assert only one guarantee that baptism itself embodies: the incomprehensible and limitless love of God for us.

Could it really be that baptism is so simple, that in the loving engagement of persons with water, one element essential to every expression of life as we know it, we embody what already is: God's unfailing love for us, and God's hunger that we live that love in loving all of creation? Why would we make it more complex? Could it be that our own penchant for making it complicated and obscure results from our desire to control? If so, we are forgetting who we are and who God is, precisely what baptism addresses.

Shall a woman forget the baby at her breast? Even should she, yet never will I forget you. *Baptizata sum.* Beloved of God, by the world-full.

CHAPTER 3

Sharing the Stuff of Life: Gathering for Meals

We are born hungry, it seems. Almost immediately after birth, we begin to take nourishment, and for many months we do so often. For most of us, mother's milk suffices for a time, but eventually cereal is added to our diet. Then all manner of foods and beverages may come tumbling in: fruits and juices in every color of the rainbow, vegetables in an astonishing circus parade of shapes and flavors, perhaps poultry, meats, and sea foods, naughty sweet treats, and all manner of breads, crackers, rolls, buns, pancakes, cookies, tortillas, cakes, pastries, and pastas.

For much of the world, a grain product—whether of wheat, corn, rice, or other grain—is the staff of life. Without it, many would hardly know how to eat. Nor can we do without plentiful liquids: six to eight glasses of water a day we should drink, the nutritionists tell us. If we want tea, milk, or juice, that's extra.

Rumor has it that we are what we eat. Some of us take that quite seriously, pondering our diet and pouring considerable time and energy into finding the healthiest foods we can, putting them together in the way most likely to enable them to enhance each other's nutrient character. Others are less interested in the long-term effects of their meals and concern themselves with delighting and astonishing taste buds trained to savor subtle nuances of flavor and texture. Such folk may live to eat rather than eating to live. Many of us use food as a tool: as a mechanism for comforting a distressed inner being, as a reward for all manner of accomplishments, as a metaphor intended to express an inclination, emotion, desire, conviction. Food clearly has more to do with life than the chemical equations between nutrients and body cells! Each particular food has astronomical potential for an incredible cascade of meanings, values, possibilities for shaping life. Lack of liked food can render us less than human almost as fast or perhaps faster than lack of sufficient food.

I hated green peas as a child. I don't understand that now, but making me eat them then was tantamount to punishment. My sister, as I recall, felt that way about liver sausage. But give her a freshly made bowl of popcorn, and she will likely feel that all is right with the world, even if all hell is breaking loose outside (I may exaggerate a trifle). As for me, well, chocolate has long been my passion—deep, dark, and bitter—the only kind there is. I think it may always have been so, for my mother hankered after chocolates and my father chocolate ice cream. But I also remember one night when I was having a very bad time of it, sent away from the dinner table for some misdemeanor I'm sure was my sister's, when my father came into my room to give me the chocolate frosting from the top of his dessert cupcake. It did seem then that there truly was justice in the world, and that my father really did love me.

It is not only the food itself that matters, but particular occasions surrounding consumption and the patterns of eating ingrained in us. Perhaps the most prevalent pattern is the practice of eating in the company of others, sharing food together. Basic human needs around hunger and thirst are accompanied by the need for companionship, *cum* + *panis*, or "breading together."[1] Even many who live alone tend to eat in the company of television newscasters or electronically present sisters and brothers of the human family.

Common Patterns

Every society has meal-sharing traditions. At birthdays in the house in which I grew up, the birthday person always got to decide on the menu for the whole family. Yet, I cannot remember a time when we did not have a birthday cake replete with candles for wishing over and blowing out. Family reunions and church suppers were always potluck. Elsewhere covered-dish suppers prevail. In my Long Island congregation I encountered the progressive dinner; in Canada, fowl suppers and Linger Lunches. The name and manner of gathering changes, but the fact of gathering to share meals is probably as ancient as the human species.

Such gatherings are foundational in the biblical traditions. Within the Older Testament, we find multiple meal stories, each carrying far more freight than the food on the table. The announcement of Sarah's pregnancy

---

[1]John E. Burkhart, *Worship: A Searching Examination of the Liturgical Experience* (Philadelphia: Westminster Press, 1982), 76.

occurs at a meal, and the exodus people gathered for meals of quail and manna. Wisdom's feast (Proverbs 9:1–5) tempts us, as do Sabbath meals and harvest festivals, along with many more occasions of *cum panis,* table sharing. Food also could be given as a gift or made into a cultic offering, or it could serve as metaphor for other realities of life. Bread, the staff of life for Hebrew communities, provides a good example. The enemy as bread is easily conquered, the bread of deceit is falsehood, while the bread of tears is the essence of sorrow (Psalm 80:5). The bread of idleness means the substance or fruit of sloth (Proverbs 31:27), and the bread of adversity equals the essence or fruit of trouble (Isaiah 30:20). Bread can also represent wisdom (Proverbs 9:5) and the true word of God (Isaiah 55:2).

People in the Hellenistic Greek world in which Jesus lived regularly participated in associations called *koinonia* groups for meals and conversation. While the Jewish Sabbath meal took place in the context of the family, an ordinary *koinonia* meal might not be familial at all, and in fact, could include people from a variety of different stations in life.[2]

Perhaps some of the meals Jesus participated in were these, thus earning him the accusation of being a glutton and drunkard. Yet scripture describes many other occasions of meals with Jesus: in the home of Mary and Martha, with a crowd of strangers around loaves and fish, at Zaccheus' house, for example. Surely, in several years of Jesus' wanderings, many people had opportunity to engage in table companionship, *cum panis,* with Jesus.

I suspect those meals carried all the flavors of relationship to which we are accustomed. I imagine Mary was never happy about how rarely Jesus came home for dinner and worried if he was eating right. No doubt, questions about his overall welfare, whom he was seeing, the crowd he ran with, and what might become of him were discussed at table both when Jesus was present and when he was not. Meals with Jesus surely included casual chatter, much laughter, arguments, teasing, and times when nobody talked very much at all, because all were caught up in their own thoughts or too peeved with one another to care to speak with each other. Surely theological discussions of all kinds occurred, and plans for the next day or the next week were made. I imagine people were comforted, invited to tell their story, asked how their day went, asked what they thought about the current political situation. I expect people complained about the food or raved about it, discussed who wanted the last olive or piece of fish, who would wash the dishes, and who would do the

---

[2]Burton L. Mack, *A Myth of Innocence: Mark and Christian Origins* (Minneapolis: Fortress Press, 1988, 1991), 81–82, 101–102.

shopping for the next meal. And I would like to believe that when Jesus had his way, no one—not women, not children, not strangers, not pariahs, not the least of these my sisters, brothers—was ever excluded.

Going Hungry

We can probably safely assume bread was broken and eaten at all these meals as a regular part of eating together. That scripture uses "breaking bread" as a metaphor for worship gatherings of the early church (Acts 2:42, 46; 20:7) implies that sharing meals together, probably ordinary meals, was fundamental to the worship life of early Christians. We are probably safe in assuming that often when early Christian groups gathered they gathered for a shared meal and talked about Jesus. These may have been the occasions when those gathered most concretely experienced the presence of God as they had experienced it when Jesus was at table with them. Still, before much time at all had passed, Paul, anxious to correct the Corinthians' poor table hospitality, speaks of having "received from the Lord" [sic] (1 Corinthians 11:23) a specific perspective on the church's meals, a perspective in which the bread commonly shared is now seen as the body of Christ and the cup as the cup of a new covenant. The Synoptic Gospels next recite similar stories clearly intended to explain the roots of the church's meal. Meanwhile, the author of the Gospel of John offers what I perceive to be a countertext that speaks of Jesus himself as the true (spiritual) meal (John 6:31–35), perhaps pursuing Paul's claim that in breaking bread we participate in the body of Christ (1 Corinthians 10:16).

What each of these texts likely offers is a particular group's impression of what their common meals were about. Thus, these are narratives of *interpretation*[3] rather than the narratives of institution the church has defined them to be. Moreover, the notion that Jesus instituted such a ritual meal is a later invention probably intended to baptize as particularly Christian the common practice of the *koinonia* meal.

Sadly, before too long, the practice and notion of that meal being a real meal vanished, impossible to sustain perhaps where persecution existed, or under pressure from a highly stratified social structure, or in the face of growing crowds of Christians. Or perhaps it simply fell under the control of ritualizers. Meanwhile, theology, too, lost track of the radical social character of meals with Jesus and then struggled to work out metaphysically the exact equation between Christ and what had become "holy

---

[3]In courses I co-taught with Stephen Farris, he repeatedly, and rightly, emphasized this distinction.

food."[4] As well, a resurgence of sacrificial thinking and excessive clericalism so far removed the now ritual act from ordinary table-sharing that, to this day, most of us have difficulty thinking of a Sunday morning event at the table as a meal. We may be starving to death as a result.

I thought I was starving for want of access to the table in those years I was an itinerant preacher, going here of a Sunday and there of a Sunday to "fill the pulpit" for absent pastors. These were good, caring churches that followed the leftover reformation pattern of having communion four times a year.[5] Communion Sundays varied from church to church, and somehow it seemed I was always preaching in a congregation that had communion last week when I was somewhere else. At least I could make sure the preaching was an event full of gospel, but I also needed to experience the gift of the table, *cum panis*.

Even when I moved on to full-time doctoral studies, I found that while I might have easier access to the table, what happened there was usually so sterile that, for all I knew what I could *hope* to experience there, and for all the words said about that, I was hard-pressed to make anything more of the wafer or pinch and sip or dip than a pitiful parody of an impoverished feast. Nor did this problem resolve when congregations adopted "eucharistic prayers" that often function like second sermons, and replaced receiving the elements in the pews with queuing up like consumers at their favorite fast-food restaurant. What kind of *cum panis* is this?

Setting the Table Anew

Yet John Calvin believed we needed access to the table weekly, so that we might see, feel, taste, smell the substance of God's incredible love for us as a counter to the very tangible presence of hatred and horror in the world.[6] He insisted also that we need real correspondence between the symbol and that which it signifies.[7] If we are to speak of bread, if we are to engage with bread, we must be able to know by looking, touching, smelling, tasting it that it is in fact the staff of life and not something else. What then of loaves denuded of their crust and diced, of loaves shredded

---

[4]Notions of transubstantiation and consubstantiation, as well as Zwingli's insistence that the elements of bread and cup are only signs, and Calvin's naming of Christ's presence as context rather than content all reflect this struggle.

[5]In fact John Calvin wanted communion celebrated weekly in Geneva. The town fathers refused to permit this. The later Reformed Mercersburgers, Philip Schaff and John Nevin, also were unsuccessful in opening the Reformed churches to this practice.

[6]*Institutes,* 4.17.8.

[7]*Institutes,* 4.17.14.

by the tiniest of pinches, of bland wafers that stick like glue to the roof of one's mouth and taste like glue? What then of eating on the run, one by one, each of us getting our tiny dollop like so many Oliver Twists, each one having a little personal communion? Please, may I have some more? Am I the only one dying for want of a fulsome meal with God who, as Calvin put it, feeds us like a loving parent,[8] hungering to provide us three nutritious meals a day? Am I the only one dying for the wonderful exchange of relationship at the family table at the best of times and maybe even at the worst of times?

What do we need when we gather around the table? I dare say we need a vigorous sharing of gifts of food and drink sufficient to enable us to unmistakably experience the extraordinary love of God for us, love that was paradigmatically embodied in the words/deeds/death/resurrection of Christ Jesus. I think we need the profound engagement of looking after one another's needs, of hand-to-hand and body-to-body seeing that each one of us has enough to eat and drink. Well fed—in whatever condition we come—with the ordinary stuff of life, caught up in the lively interchange surrounding a common table where each ensures the other is well looked after, we can know our Faithful Nurturer's love for us is as basic and essential as bread and the quenching of thirst and as personal as our individual being. God's love experienced at such a table can bring us alive in love—individually and as a community, no matter what we have done or left undone. At the same time, that love calls us to embrace the challenge of embodying love toward others and thus toward God. How else shall we eat when two thirds of the world goes without adequate nutrition except by committing ourselves to find potent ways to nourish the hungry?

What's in a Name?

I prefer to call this event "the meal." True, there are many other names in the tradition,[9] but all are so unique to Christianity that they allow us to think of Christianity as a private club that engages in an exclusive ritual peculiar to its initiates. "The meal" brings us back not only to the many meals Jesus shared with intimates and strangers, but also to the basic reality of human hunger and thirst, to the daily need to eat and drink in company, to the recognition that in our creatureliness and quite without regard to creed or faith tradition, all people are our sisters and brothers, equally loved by God, equally in need of *cum panis,* companionship, breading

---

[8] *Institutes,* 4.17.1.

[9] Lord's supper, breaking of bread, eucharist (good gifts; thanksgiving), memorial, sacrifice, table sharing, communion, holy communion.

together for our joint survival, growth, and life. Moreover, Augustine understood that eating together makes us bread for the world, food and drink for others, family, strangers, or friends—whether they are Christian or not. "There you are on the table,"[10] he said, speaking to the community inclusive of the newly baptized, speaking of the loaf and cup they are about to share. It is almost as if he is saying, "Become what you are meant to be," the bread, the cup, active participants in the body of Christ, a gift of love[11] in and for the life of the world. Perhaps we would do better to say, "there you are *around* the table, become what you are meant to be"!

The food we share and the sharing of food when the Christian community gathers are intimately related to the bread we eat at home, our eating of bread at our community lunch or potluck supper, the food at the food bank and grocery store, and the grains distributed to the victims of famine and war. The cup we share and the drinking of the cup, when the Christian community gathers are intimately related with the beverages served at home, to our gathering around the punch bowl, to the dehydrated children of Rwanda, and the IV drip of the hospitalized.

Multiple Embodiments

There are may ways to embody gospel and to experience gospel bodied forth. One of the richest of them is by gathering regularly at Christ's table, if what we do there ours for witnesses fully the reality of God's abundant love for us *and* ours for all God's creation. We will want to ensure that the food is substantial enough to reveal the essence of life that Christ is. At least for many in our Western culture, we are talking about real bread made of flour and water and perhaps sugar and yeast, kneaded, left to rise in a warm place, baked at 300 degrees and more. Smell the rich aroma permeating the whole house of your memory, the household of God! See coming out of the oven or bread machine the loaf richly encrusted and all of it of a piece, bread that embodies nourishment, empowerment for being, life. No separate grains of flour, these, but a gathered, connected, diversity of flour, salt, water, perhaps herbs, fruits, or nuts in unity. Meant to feed the hungry, nurture the weak, sustain the strong, this stuff of life brings with it deep sensory memories of a thousand meals shared, savory occasions of rice liberally seasoned with laughter as well as tears, of corn

---

[10]Sermon 229, "On the Sacraments of the Faithful," in *Fathers of the Church*, vol. 38, tr. Sister Mary Sarah Muldowney, R.S.M. (New York: Fathers of the Church, 1959). See also Luther, "The Adoration of the Sacrament," *Luther's Works*, vol. 36 (Philadelphia: Muhlenberg Press, 1959), 287.

[11]Luther, "the fruit of the sacrament...is nothing other than love." "Against the Fanatics," *LW* 36, 352.

lovingly, patiently ground for a crowd, patted into shape, baked; of bread dipped, used as a spoon; of grains gathering to them vegetables and spices; of everyday and special meals each empowering us so that we in turn might be "bread" for the world. Surely you are hungry for this "bread"!

The bread we share need not be wheat bread, but what embodies for the community the stuff/staff of life. Cultural heritage matters here, since God relates with us where *we* are. So does allergy—it is hard to share in a meal of life if the contents of the meal are toxic! More and more we will need to broaden our concept of "one loaf" to include a bountiful measure of "staffs (staves?) of life"—rice crackers, wheat pitas, corn tortillas, eggless/milkless/butterless breads—and find our symbol of unity *in the care-filled sharing of the meal* rather than in the particularity of the food.

The same is true for the cup, which needs only be filled with liquid sufficient to quench thirst and enliven us. Perhaps for us the contents of the cup will rightly be water, clean and pure, an even rarer commodity than ever before, and no less essential to human being. Such water readily promises the ongoing gift of life to us and through us to those who do not now have safe water to drink. Perhaps one cup may in fact be two or four, each filled with a drink that gives life—water, milk, or milk and honey, fruit of the vine, or juices of other fruits, or wine made from rice—to be chosen by meal participants according to need and desire. This seems to have been done before,[12] and surely we, too, can find our unity in the sharing with each according to her or his needs rather than in some singular, exclusive content.

The elements finally do not matter so much, although I agree with Calvin that they ought demonstrate to every sense what they are meant to do. But the *way* God's life-giving gifts are shared matters a great deal. Does the act of *cum panis* take precedence over talking about it? Do we carry out this meal in such a manner that it truly *embodies* gospel—God's freely given gift of love that embraces us in dialogical relationship with God and neighbor? Do strangers feel really welcome? Do we offer enough

---

[12]Justin speaks of a cup of water *and of* mixed wine, and of giving out bread *and* wine *and* water in chapter 65 of his "First Apology," *Early Christian Fathers,* Vol. I, *Library of Christian Classics,* Cyril C. Richardson, ed. (Philadelphia: Westminster Press, 1953) and again in chapter 67, says bread *and* wine *and* water are brought to the presider. Some communities, e.g., The *Hydro-parastatæ* Encratites, used water alone. Cyprian argued against this practice with an astonishingly strained topological proof-texting. "The Epistles of Cyprian: To Cæcilius, on the Sacrament of the Cup of the Lord," *The Ante-Nicene Fathers,* Alexander Roberts and James Donaldson, eds. (Edinburgh: T&T Clark/Grand Rapids: Wm. B. Eerdmans Publishing Company, 1990), 359ff. The so-called Apostolic Tradition of Hippolytus includes a cup of milk mixed with honey as part of the meal. G. J. Cuming, ed. *Hippolytus: A Text for Students* (Bramcote Notts: Grove Press, 1976), 21.

in variety and quantity to satisfy hunger and thirst? Do we risk taking more than a pinch and a dip or sip so we might more truly experience the abundance of Divine love for us? Do we meet each other face to face, get to know each other better, attend faithfully to the needs of all who come, whether we fully understand them or not?

If we hear the words of Paul to our kin at Corinth, if we embrace gospel, we will be free to seek a manner of inviting people to and participating in the meal that embodies love, that builds community, that empowers the whole gathering to bring the bread of life and the cup of new covenant community into a world in desperate need. Perhaps when we participate in that meal we would do well to *all* bring bread and grapes, tortillas, cold spring water, to proclaim the abundance of God's love for all and to take to those who have none. Perhaps we need to take up an entirely different pattern. I think of the AME Zion congregation that years ago invited me to preach. Their service always was followed with a meal, and although there were particular words that concluded one and words that began the other, it was abundantly clear to me that worship didn't end before lunch to which everyone was invited. Similarly, a Methodist congregation I knew offered, following their monthly communion service, a lunch for all in the wider community who were hungry. Such patterns could help us remember that at every meal God and all God's family are our companions, and that God nourishes us so that we may feed the world.

And yet, will we not also need to ask how a formal communion during the worship hour differs from the common meal that follows it (after a benediction and another table blessing!) in the fellowship hall? Are these not truly the same gift, only done twice, once formally, the other more likely with heart, gaiety, and much intercommunication and relationship that lives out the memory/presence of Christ in our midst? How might we most faithfully participate in holy communion, that deep, life-giving relationship with the One who loves us beyond our imagining and powers our love for one another and the world?

CHAPTER 4

The Possibility of Prayer

We begin with deep breathing. Locating ourselves in a comfortable place, we stop all intentional activity and take in a slow, deep breath. We feel the breath follow the beckoning of the diaphragm and flood our inner self. Expanded, and a tiny bit exhilarated, we relax, releasing the breath, breathing deeply again. Now the breath burrows deeper, down to the pelvic cradle where it rests just for the wink of an eye, before we relax, releasing the breath back to the world. The breath floods in again like the waves of the sea, flowing joyfully to the tips of our toes, curling around them and ebbing away as we relax and exhale. We follow new breath down to our toes again and way up around the nooks and crannies of our brains and relax, releasing, breathing, relaxing, in the breath, buoyed up by it, supported by it as it ebbs and flows…In time we find ourselves be-calmed, resting on the breath in the center of our being. There we are safe, at home, where God dwells. We rest, too, in the heart of God, where we dwell, within the Breath of Life…

I learned to pray, or so I thought, by rote. "Now I lay me down to sleep…;""Come, Lord [sic] Jesus, be thou our guest…;""Our Father [sic], who art in heaven…" But then, suddenly (or so it seems now) I was a pastor and responsible for leading in prayer well beyond what I had been taught. All that memorization went for nought. I had learned something from hearing others pray, but how much of what I had learned was helpful is another question entirely. Sunday morning was coming up momen-tarily. How would we pray?

The church secretary kept a file of all the old Sunday bulletins. I could just pull out the prayer from last year, or, if that didn't quite suit, the year before. That's what they'd done before I got there. But it set my teeth on edge. Part of the problem was that the prayers belonged to the past

—they didn't address the reality of this congregation *now*. At least I had the good sense to know that. But there I was, bestowed with the M.Div. degree, ordained, pastoring, and I really didn't know how to pray.

I probably began by altering last year's prayers, at which point the poet in me rose up in outright rebellion. I could write more fitting prayers than these if I prayed the day's texts a while and let them pray in me; if I then just sat down at the keyboard and let the muse dance through my fingers, putting down words that came from a place deep within, a place about which I really knew nothing. The congregation loved those prayers, so they said. I was never sure if it was because they loved the poetry or because the poetry enabled them to pray. Perhaps both.

Unfortunately, that process didn't work very well for extemporaneous praying. Not my gift, I said. But then my students wanted me to teach them to pray. It's not enough to tell them to live with the text for a while and then sit down at the keyboard and let the words flow through their fingers from some deep place they know nothing about. And yet...

God's Gift/Human Response

In classical theology, prayer is predicated on grace: We pray because God makes the divine self accessible to us. Augustine suggests the heart is restless until it rests in God. Either the restlessness is stirred up by God—who hungers for us to come to the divine self—or God makes the divine self known to us over against our restlessness so we *can* turn to the One who beckons us. Indeed, is not the situation both/and? God *is* there for us, as is evident in the faith claims of the Hebrew people, whose impassioned, daily prayer life we discover in the psalms. Christ Jesus, in bodying forth love to confused, sick, hungry, and desperate folk, also poignantly manifests God's presence for us. God *is* there for us. How odd, then, that our prayers seem always to begin with words, *our* words.

We pray because the One who loves us lets us know that the divine self is accessible to us, because somehow we hear God-for-us calling us amid the babble of our life, because amid the chaos of our existence we feel the countermovement of God-with-us. Could we even cry out in our despair, pain, or confusion if God did not make the divine self available to us? What else does it mean to call God "creator," "source of life," "sustainer—*breath*—of life"? We can pray not only because of our need, but because God lets us know that God is there for us, if only by creating in us hope against hope that God *will* be there for us. Prayer begins with God, and on our part, the silence of breathing in, with, and through the Spirit.

Paul says we do not even know how to pray (Romans 8:26). How well I know! We do not have the thoughts, we do not have the words, only the need. So it is not only *that* we can pray that is gift, but the prayers themselves are gift—sometimes only "sighs too deep for words." God's own Spirit within us, knowing every nook and cranny of our being, brings us and God together in the other-consciousness of prayer. None of us know how to pray—even the disciples had to be taught. If they, who walked, talked, laughed, and ate daily with Jesus needed instruction, how will any of us pray except that the Spirit of God move in us, breathe in us? How odd that our "prayers" always begin with words, *our* words!

Prayer is predicated on grace, on the presence of the Compassionate One within us, breathing life in us, prompting us where needed, pouring words, sometimes, through fingers from deep recesses of our being. Yet even if our only words are "O, God!" the very fact that we call out, that we address God, honors God, suggests Luther.[1] Such a cry acknowledges our hunger for One who will be for us, who *is* for us; it reveals transcendence of our fierce independence and our hope for and openness to life-giving relationship—exactly that with which God seeks to grace us.

Luther also tells us that our loving Friend commands us to pray—and what is that but a promise to attend our prayers?[2] Perhaps God invites us to pray because God needs ego strokes, but I am more persuaded that God invites us to pray so that we will know our prayer is urgently wanted, that God hungers to be in conversation with us, and that God will respond—that we might "know" in our bones that God lives with us. Surely such an invitation promises that God is not immutable, but is moved by our prayers, and will hear, feel, answer them. Could a mother who cannot forget us ignore us? Could the one who embraces us in loving, dialogical relationship, who nourishes us at table, breathes in us, dwells in us turn a deaf ear to our efforts at conversation? Still, prayer is not magic and does not achieve what we want just by virtue of shaping the thought or words, let alone merely by reciting them. God is not a good fairy or a television or web-accessed Celestial Home Shopping Service!

So Luther can say that for "true prayer there must be earnestness,"[3] and Karl Barth that where there is no heart, there is no prayer.[4] "The

---

[1] "The Large Catechism," *The Book of Concord: The Confessions of the Evangelical Lutheran Church,* tr., ed. Theodore G. Tappert (Philadelphia: Fortress Press, 1959), 421.

[2] "The Large Catechism," 420–21, 423.

[3] "The Large Catechism," 423.

[4] Karl Barth, *Prayer,* ed. Don E. Saliers, tr. Sara F. Terrien (Philadelphia: Westminster Press, 1985), 39.

hardened heart does not pray,"[5] says my friend and colleague Don Saliers (yet, I wonder if any hearts are so hard that they cannot be moved by the effervescence of God within?). Augustine suggests prayer is "a turning of the heart" to God so that we are ready to receive what God gives.[6] In our need comes a turning, and in the turning, a melting of the heart? My experience confirms this. So Luther writes: "God therefore wishes you to lament and express your needs and wants, not because God is unaware of them, but in order that you may kindle your heart to stronger and greater desires and spread your cloak wide to receive many things."[7] What things? Opinions vary, but one thing holds firm for me. Prayer *does* effect something that we need, something God knows we need even if we never know it ourselves, even if we never get the right words out, even if we never get the words out at all. Prayer effects relationship anew. It "works" because God remains always in loving relationship with us; because God breathes in us, experiences, and ever faithfully responds to the passion of our hearts.

Prayer as Solidarity

This may not seem enough when the Red River floods, or the prairies choke in dust, and the wheat refuses to grow; when mines cave in and the cod or salmon fisheries dry up, when the rate of unemployment only goes up and never down, when children sniff gasoline, or wind up prostituting or murdering themselves on the streets. Understandably so. There are times when I lose all interest in relationship; I just want God to fix things. What must this be like for those who are not as privileged as I, whose whole lives are lived amid unrelenting squalor or in unremitting agony? Such questions have a long history. For me, a beginning answer lies in the fact that prayer starts with recognition of the Other who resides both within and without, whose never-failing presence is fluid, dynamic, intimate with us like the very air we breathe. We breathe the breath that belongs to God, that God gives us to bring us alive, keep us alive. We do not own this breath; it is ours to share. When we breathe, we breathe with the cosmos, we breathe the breath that has crisscrossed the globe, breath inhaled and exhaled by brothers in Newfoundland and Tanzania, by sisters in Chile and Mongolia, by green things in Central or Stanley Park, and creatures hidden in deserts and not-so-hidden in forests and prairies.

---

[5]Don E. Saliers, "Prayer and Emotion: Shaping and Expressing Christian Life," *Christians at Prayer*, ed. John Gallen, S.J., (Notre Dame: University of Notre Dame Press, 1977), 46.

[6]"Our Lord's Sermon on the Mount," *The Preaching of Augustine*, ed. Jaroslav Pelikan, tr. Francine Cardman (Philadelphia: Fortress Press, 1973), 3.15, 105.

[7]"The Large Catechism," 424.

The breath of God has never been limited to the Garden of Eden or Ezekiel's valley, but God gives it universally, breathes it, shares it.

Nor do we own the prayer that breath speaks in us and through us. Like our very breath, prayer is not a private matter, a hermetically sealed correspondence with God. As members of God's beloved family of friends, each of us indwelt with Holy Spirit, we pray with all who have ever prayed or will pray. Our prayer is neither prayed alone, nor does it have to do with only ourselves. Prayer is a matter of our relationship not only with God, but also with all God's global family. Even when we pray for ourselves and when we pray in our closet, in the same way that we share in breathing, we pray in solidarity with all who need God's tender loving care. The prayer we call Jesus' own is a corporate prayer—*our* parent, give *us our* daily bread, forgive *us* as *we* forgive, lead *us* not, deliver *us*. This prayer is prayer for the world,[8] having to do with the call and the ability to love God and our neighbor as ourselves. Indeed, all prayer has to do with our global community, and all prayer, in some way, embraces all humanity in relationship with God.

Radical Business

Prayer is not, then, only discourse with God, but commitment to the world full of God's beloved people. When we recognize our very breath is shared round the world, that ought to make us think about what we do to keep that breath-to-be-shared fresh and viable. When we ask for the economy of God to be known, we ask not for our private blessing, but for the life of the world. At the same time we commit ourselves to participating in a ministry of manifesting that reality in the world. When we seek bread for ourselves, we do so for all hungry people, and we commit ourselves to take a meaningful part in feeding the world. We already know this. We see it at work in the Canadian Foodgrains Bank, in Out of the Cold programs, in hay trucked south of the border to meet a desperate need, or in wheat shuttled halfway around the world to help end the next famine. The same is true for all our prayers. When we pray for forgiveness for ourselves, we petition the same for the world; we commit ourselves to forgive the world and to work for reconciliation and peace everywhere. When we ask for release from pain or horror, we take on responsibility to liberate our brothers and sisters from misery and angst. Prayer, like breathing (!), is radical business. It belongs to and effects living out loving, dialogical relationship with God and neighbor. Blessed with God-for-us,

---

[8] *Institutes* 3.20, 34–47.

prayer expects us to embody gospel, the love of God to and for others, with as much dailyness as our daily breath.

Planning Ahead

With every breath we take, we are engaged in theology—how else could we describe breathing as participating with others in the life-breath of God? Everything we say and do in prayer, and most especially in public prayer, says or does something of gospel. When we take responsibility for the public speaking of prayer, then, we need to prepare. The preparation of deep breathing helps equip us to experience anew God's giving of Godself to us and our relationship with the whole of our cosmos. Listening as we breathe, we hope to hear the prayers of the cosmos, the needs of God's global family, the rustle of Divine Wind in places in the world we might never have expected. Such prayers as we might then shape will be rooted in our reality as well as in our vision. We will be able to find and use language that will say concretely what it means and will intentionally embrace all kinds of people in love. Above all, our prayer will aim to shift the balance of power in the world toward life for all creation.

As well, we who pray publicly need remember that the prayers we speak forth, like all of worship and preaching, belong to all the congregation. For all that individuals may do much of the preparation and the speaking, prayer leaders *pray with* the people in the pew, not on their behalf. We can enhance prayer life by increasing opportunities for persons at worship events to speak prayers, even if those prayers stumble, even if the one who speaks puts her foot in her mouth, even if the prayers sometimes sound like sermons-in-disguise. Perfection in prayer is not required, and it is not possible. What is received by God is the passion of the heart, the sighs of the spirit. That is what we, too, are freed to hear and what we are invited to stand in solidarity with and commitment to: the anguish and the need and, yes, the exuberance and joy.

The people of a congregation can learn to create all of a worship event's prayers, prayers that grow out of the people's experience of gospel intersecting with their particular reality. After engaging with an upcoming Sunday's texts and event design,[9] small groups of people (including children!) are able to create splendid gathering prayers, prayers of confession, thanksgiving prayers, prayers that grow out of the interaction between the text and their experience, prayers that reflect their reality, their need, their hopes in the light of the gospel of that particular day. This is so because God is there for them, because they can listen in silence or through

---

[9]See chapter 14 for more specific address of this.

movement to the word of scripture and the need of the world, because God empowers everyone's prayers. These prayers can be shared with the rest of the community of a Sunday morning because multiple representatives of the community created them in part out of diverse experiences with and perspectives on the larger community, and because next week or next month another group can take a turn. Eventually, I am convinced, as more and more members of congregations participate in crafting such prayers in advance, more and more will grow in the depth and impact of their own prayer life and in their ability to pray life into the world. Some will even evolve into gifted extemporaneous pray-ers, and all will likely discover greater comfort in both silent and voiced prayer.

Even if this does not occur, the norm of preachers and presiders praying prayers they have borrowed or constructed on their own on behalf of the people can no longer endure. Life with God is corporate life, and all need to share in the power of giving expression to the depths and heights of that relationality. So worship leaders need to help encourage and enable Christians to pray publicly so prayers of the people will be truly the people's prayers.

A Step-by-Step Process

We can begin, as the chapter began, with breathing and allowing the life-breath we all share, the movement of God within, to center and focus us in silence. Someone can then read aloud the key text for the day at a pace gentle enough to surface images, metaphors, ideas, needs in the sensory systems of group members. These can then be shared verbally, but groups will greatly enrich their experience if they risk moving their inner event. Participants might act out parts of the text or their sensory experience or mime it; they might try and figure out what fear, uncertainty, or relief "looks like walking around," or what movements in their daily life seem somehow to express something of the text. Diversity will likely sound a strong chord here, but an amazing sense of wholeness and community has resulted from every experience of this in which I have participated.

The group may wish to engage in the same activity with supporting texts, identifying common threads or patterns as well as gaps and disagreements between texts. Next, the group can identify contextual realities of all kinds: personal, communal, global, liturgical, etc. What is going on with whom? In what way might the text(s) impact these? What kinds of prayers can address these realities within the worship event: in an opening prayer, a thanksgiving prayer, a prayer at the table or font, etc.? Such prayers might have a particular purpose such as adoration, confession, thanks, intercession, petition. Once the purpose and general content of a prayer is clear, what kind of structure or form does it want? How will it begin and end? What will happen in between?

From this point on, it is a matter of weaving the words together to do what the prayer needs. Some do this best aloud, others on paper or keyboard and screen. In either case, if the prayer is going to be spoken aloud, it needs to be tested that way. Does the prayer move coherently? Will people be able to hear it if they don't see it in print? speak it aloud if they are invited to do so? Will it enable them to pray, to truly engage in relationship with God and cosmos or merely to recite words?

There are many faithful ways to pray, but when, in workshops, I have asked people what helps them pray, they propose the following characteristics or qualities of prayer:

- Remember with whom you are conversing and why.
- Use short, succinct sentences or easily followed poetry.
- Use contemporary, daily language.
- Be sensitive to the diversity of realities, views, needs within community and world.
- Use concrete, vivid images rather than abstract concepts or "universal" ideas.
- Stick to the point (don't digress or obstruct flow).
- Avoid "sermonizing."
- Don't attempt to include everything—a prayer is only *one* piece of a worship event.
- Avoid jargon (ecclesiology, soteriology, along with standard but worn-out prayer phrases).
- Mean what you say or don't say it.
- Leave plenty of silent spaces for others to add their own praying.

All need freedom to express the affection of the heart that is first God's gift to us; all need guidance in participating in this conversation with God and world *because* it constitutes relationship with God and world *anew*. If we seek such transformed life in prayer, a life of loving, dialogical relationship with God and neighbor, we will move the Rockies and the Alps if need be to participate in God's gift and to be accountable to God's gift so that our prayers personal and communal bring us life and give life to the world. And let us not forget the silence! Breathe in us, breath of God!

CHAPTER 5

Embodied Preaching

Then the word of God came to Elijah, saying, "Go now to Zarephath and live there; for I have commanded a widow there to feed you." So Elijah went. When he came to the gate of the town, a widow was there gathering sticks. Elijah called to her, "Bring me a little water in a vessel so that I may drink. Bring me a morsel of bread in your hand." But she said, "I have nothing baked, only a handful of meal in a jar, and a little oil in a jug; I am gathering sticks so that I may go home and prepare it for myself and my child, that we may eat it and die." Elijah said to her, "First make me a little cake and bring it to me, and afterwards make something for yourself and your child. For thus says the God of Israel:, The jar of meal will not be emptied and the jug of oil will not fail until the day that God sends rain on the earth." She did as Elijah said. The jar of meal never emptied, neither did the jug of oil fail (1 Kings 17:8–16 NRSV, adapted).

We feel the rhythms, the rhythm of the diaphragmatic wailing of a hungry child, the rhythm of rocking in despair, the rhythm of sluggish, weary walking, of hypoglycemic shaking, of picking up sticks, of bend and reach and step and bend and reach and step. We sense the motion of putting one foot in front of the other, of shimmering mirage, of labored, dehydrated breathing, of slogging out of the wilderness, of a bucket being hand-over-handed up the well, of ill-advised gulping of water down a parched and sore throat. Our muscles contract and release through the day-after-day going to the cupboard, in reaching up and bringing down the jug and then the jar, in kneading and pouring, in giving and taking, in chewing and swallowing.

We move the rhythm of questions asked and answered, of pour and dip and wash; we sense the motion of gathering Sunday by Sunday; we feel the flow of hymn and prayer, the contract/release of work and play, the up, down, in, and out of life in the global community. The movement goes on without end in endless variation. The movement is the motion of God being there for us, the rhythm of God embodied for us in mothers who give us shelter, who rock us to sleep, who keep us clean, and dry, and fed. The movement is the kinesthesia of God embodied in prophets who call us to account and envision our future; of God embodied in helpless infants whose only talent seems to be coaxing an impossible smile out of us as we reach beyond ourselves to be whatever they need us to be.

Left to our self-sufficiency, we would all be dead. But God is there for us, the Prime Mover moving in pastors and pew-sitters, parents and children, neighbors and strangers from distant lands; God embodied in everyone who lives only a face, a hand, a heart of God away from death; God embodied in everyone whose face, hands, heart stand between us and death.

Message or Event?

I have trouble making the transition from hearing a sermon on Sunday morning to living gospel all the rest of the week. If the truth be known, I often have trouble hearing sermons at all, even though I am a preacher, or perhaps because I am a preacher. In any case, words, concepts, appeals to intellect so common in preaching, even stories, no matter how wonderful, are rarely enough for me to hang on to, let alone act upon. Not only in my moments of deepest distress have I needed more than wonderful words of love. I have needed God embodied in hands that bathed me, hands that put bread in my hands; I have needed God embodied in arms that held me together and held me up; I have needed God embodied in a nod of a head that could assure me from across the room that I am still God's beloved. I have needed and daily need God embodied for me. I am not alone in this.

A theology that claims communication begins with sound originating in God's saying via *dabar* and *logos*[1] has enamored us of the word. Bolstered by the printing press and rationalism, this theology shapes a worship praxis that reveals itself to be caught up in a love affair between the intellect and the oral/aural. In Protestant worship events this word-infatuation surfaces most clearly in the dominance of preaching and in an

---

[1]John 1:1; Arthur Van Seters, "Preaching as an Oral/Aural Act," *Papers of the Annual Meeting of the Academy of Homiletics*, 1989.

astonishing verbosity of prayer.[2] Perhaps our majoring in words is one reason many accuse Christians of not practicing what we preach (pray). If our speaking is not consciously and intentionally grounded in our bodily experience, can our words be much more than empty?

Immediately, we hear a voice crying out about the objective truth of some words or the absolute truth of gospel, which stands on its own as valid apart from our behavior. Yet words are never objective and neither is gospel. Both have to do with communication between beings, whole persons engaged in relationships with other embodied individuals. Words and gospel have to do with subjectivity: God and humankind, you and I, interrelating as subjects. Nevertheless, how quickly we overlook the "angel" who wrestled with Jacob and the word embodied in the prophets. How quickly we forget how busy our bodies are in face-to-face conversation—to say nothing of incarnation, of God embodied in the loving interaction of humans at wells and tombs, at table and font, in hospital room and food bank.

In our word infatuation, something essential is missing: God creating and the Spirit hovering, the deep silence of resting in God's being, the sense of human muscles being caressed, gentled, prodded into movement before a word can be pronounced or heard and probably before it can even be thought.

Inseparability

When we begin our preaching as our prayer, with deep, intentional breathing; when we attend acutely to the breath moving through us and moving us, we remember that word and act/movement cannot be addressed separately. We are embodied beings, moving somewhere, somehow, no matter how immobile we think we are. We act before we speak—if only in inhaling breath and the dropping of jaw, as we speak, thereby forming our speech out of movement. If only those whose seemingly endless read essays rolled right over me had begun with deep breathing, with intense attunement to breath generated movement, to the Spirit prompting us not just to speech, but to act! But preachers have rarely been so trained, although many have studied the mechanics of speech.

---

[2]Most of the vast collection of homiletical literature reflects this, including that of the "New Homiletic," in spite of its claims to what Eugene Lowry calls "evocation of experiential event." Eugene Lowry, *The Sermon: Dancing on the Edge of Mystery* (Nashville: Abingdon Press, 1997), 32. Some African American preaching and worship offers a notable exception, with its strong interest in emotion and its often physically rooted, whole-community activity. See, e.g., Henry H. Mitchell, *Black Preaching: The Recovery of a Powerful Art* (Nashville: Abingdon Press, 1990), Evans E. Crawford and Thomas H. Troeger, *The Hum: Call and Response in African American Preaching* (Nashville: Abingdon Press, 1995), and Melva Wilson Costen, *African American Christian Worship* (Nashville: Abingdon Press, 1993).

Most of us have yet to reconceive preaching as an event that grows out of the wholeness of being: God's, yes, but also our very subjective, nonrational and sometimes erratic, disordered, and undeniably embodied selves engaged in dynamic relationship with God and most particularly with and through God's family. Gospel calls us to proclaim gospel by acting out of what we are, the media of the Spirit and not just speakers of the gospel message, but doers of the gospel, embodiers of God through a sermon as well as in every other dimension of our Christian life. Too many of us still speak of sermon as message, as conveyer of ideas intellect to intellect. What might happen if we begin to think of sermons as doing gospel body to body, if we refused to sit quietly in the pew or stand hidden in the pulpit and asked one another to dialogue in body language?

New Directions

Some preachers and congregations have abandoned pulpits because they obstruct the full-bodied choreography of gospel dialogue. Mindful that people "process a sermon with all of themselves" from swinging foot, to back slouching into the pew, to rising eyebrows,[3] preachers try to paint pictures with words so that people will not only see the parade of feast-fare into Wisdom's house but also get a whiff or two of fragrant bread just baked and aromatic, spicy wine.[4] It is a start. But for the most part, preachers and congregations have not yet caught the spirit of the dance. Preaching still connects us mostly head-to-head, even for those who attend to intuitive patterns of working, exercise the imagination, evoke sensory stimulation, live physicality fully. Sermons, like most prayers, continue to be constructed out of the grammar and syntax of words, sentences, paragraphs (even those of us who preach in poetic mode) rather than through body experience.

Why would we possibly want to limit ourselves to such disintegrative, disembodied proclamation of gospel? Gospel has never endorsed it, if we are honest about it, and neither will increasing numbers of people in Christian congregations. Jesus did not merely talk about the realm and reign of God, he handed out bread, fish, and wine for its feast, laid hands on the sick and dying, walked as he talked, reached down and picked up children, and probably hugged those who simply needed to be loved. As contemporary people grow more and more aware of the environment and the interconnectedness of ecosystems, we grow increasingly conscious

---

[3] Troeger, "Emerging New Standards in the Evaluation of Effective Preaching," 294.
[4] Proverbs 9:1ff.

of our own personal physicality. Our days are filled with astonishing movement—handshaking, head-nodding, walking together, handing things round, digging in our gardens—an endless parade of motional interaction. Yet how little of this constructs our sermon events. Perhaps this explains why some people raised in the church vote with their feet, choosing the activity of the golf course or the tennis court or even vigorous charismatic worship to the passivity and boredom of the "mainline" pew.

Generating Preaching through Embodiedness

Disembodied gospel simply will not do. Preaching needs to become fully empowered by gospel which is itself incarnational, *generated* through the body by those who permit Spirit, gospel, self, and community to integrate—at least as fully as any of us can ever hope for. Faithful to the inevitable and indivisible whole of act/word and body/mind, we can begin and sustain each step of the sermon development process with movement in dialogue with reason. We can ask what a text does as well as what it says. Our means of discovering the answers are grounded in the wholeness of self, in breathing, moving, thinking, acting that seek to discover and feel in all our being what is happening in this text. Rather than analyzing the text in our heads, we can allow it to choreograph our bodies, acting it out, miming it, reacting physically to it. Imagine yourself in Paul's jail cell; how do you act? How does your stomach feel, Peter, as the rooster crows for the third time? Look, the women who went to the tomb have stopped on their way to tell the rest of the company what happened. There they are in that dark corner. What are they doing? You have just crashed a party and anointed that prophet, and it suddenly dawns on you what you have done. What do you do next? You are Onesimus, a slave. What does grace look like walking around in your life? Let your body tell you!

Working our way through a text in this manner and keeping always present *our* context and congregation, we can discover a gospel experience to share with the whole community. Our body movements through the text, its choreography of us, can inscribe the form, the shape of that sharing.

The point is not to turn our brains off, but to turn our bodies on, to enable our whole selves to be full partners in the relationship with God and neighbor via the text. Such preaching does not seek the banishment of the spoken word or the surrender of intellect or scholarship. It does ask for us to be accountable to incarnation, to the indwelling of the Spirit, to the movement of God through the embodied, spiritual, intellectual, emotional wholeness of human being. Such preaching also hungers for congregations to work with preachers in creating sermons that arise out of the deep movement of the text with us all.

Embodied Preaching Is Collaborative Preaching

Gospel belongs to the whole community; it is the stuff of dialogical relationship lived out body to body. A sermon also belongs to the whole community from start to finish, and the community needs, in some way, to be bodily involved in the development of the sermon from start to finish and not just sit as the recipients of the "delivery" of them. "Little children, love one another," we are told. Yet how can we do this when the world surrounding us is more than happy to eat us alive, to run us down, and leave us but a shadow on the pavement, all without even noticing? The truth can set us free—but how will it do so if it is couched in language that addresses only our intellect and does not live where we live, be that a condominium on Quebec Avenue, a shelter in Denver, or a mobile home in Memphis? How can sermons developed solely in the pastor's brain and the electronic hiccups of a computer empower us to experience a different way of life than that which the world imposes? Is it not incarnational theology that we are all about?

So, preachers and folk from the congregation meet together to actively discover together the experience the text has to offer a given community at a particular time and place. The same pattern mapped out with regard to prayer, of engaging together in the powerful act of deep breathing and the intensive work of listening to and living scripture together, serves us here. The group's constellation and flow of movements that embody the essence of the text for the community here and now can shape the sermon in its interweaving of content and form. What are the key movements? What patterns do they create? what rhythms? Is this an explosive experience, or a gentle, easy one? Are its movements small or exaggerated? Does the energy grow from a still, small voice to a raging tempest or the reverse—or does it move in waves?

Perhaps the pattern embodied by this text is expressed by startling awake to the alarm, reaching out to shut it off, rolling out of bed, and stumbling to the shower to be straightened up there, only to sit down again for breakfast or in the car. Perhaps it will map the process of a business meeting, opening, challenging and pulling this way and that as participants struggle to work through issues and solve problems. Perhaps balancing responsibility toward family with responsibility toward the world will underlie the sermon-shape or the sudden, shocking refreshment of a dive into a cold, Canadian lake on a hot, sticky day.

However the text-in-relationship-with-congregation shapes itself, its coming to life in the worship event needs to be equally eventful. Perhaps the preacher(s) or parts of the congregation will simply dance the sermon, although that is not necessarily a goal of embodied preaching. Most often the outcome will be some combination of intentional speech/act, enacted speech. The sermon may shape itself as a more traditional aural/oral event. Yet, it will be preached as well as experienced by the congregation out of the event and impact of the collaborative, embodied process. A preacher who with sermon development partners has experienced the rearrangement of reality by the phenomenon of embodying gospel will surely come into the worship event with something more than words about the text. So the whole sermon will be different than one conceived in the head, and it will look and feel different to both preacher and people in the pew. It will be gospel bodied forth in the midst of the congregation, gospel which meets and relates with the community not as message but as lived experience.

Contextual Relationships

We do not normally experience preaching in a vacuum. Sermons not only come to life—if they actually do come to life—within a congregation, but also amid offering, bath, meal, affirmation of faith, hymn, and prayer. Whatever else we intend to carry out as a gathered community around the preaching event both informs and is informed by the homiletical enterprise. So, our homiletical work needs to be conscious of the impact of its worship context from start to finish. That quite predictably means that we attend to the character of the whole of worship not just in our heads but in our muscles, bones, nerve endings. What will be the kinesthesia of this gathering when we meet for prayer and song, word/act, conversation/choreography?

Here we may have much help by virtue of the fact that we already come together, we stand up, sit down, perhaps kneel, process up or down the aisle, or reach out to greet one another with the handclasp or hug of peace. We may dance together the choreography of baptism or meal. Our diaphragms flex as we sing and our toes may tap. Movement and worship events are no strangers, and the way in which we do things of a Sunday morning—greet one another, confess our sin, receive again the declaration of pardon, read and hear scripture, affirm our faith—all are acts that affect a sermon. On the other hand, these familiar, patterned actions may be a hindrance for their actuality carries with it all sorts of presuppositions. What might happen if we were to permit the choreography of the text-into-sermon to shape anew the giving of loaf and cup? What if we let it redesign the giving of peace, reconfigure the baptismal event, move the processional differently? Sermon development of this kind easily feeds not only the creation of prayers, but entire worship events,[5] even as prayer needs will participate in the shaping of the sermon as we attend to the interrelationship between community and text.

Perhaps this day the sequence of liturgical steps will flow directly from sermon to supper or baptism without pausing for hymn, or affirmation of faith, or taking up the collection, or any of the other many elements which may normally occur between. Perhaps the sermon will be so informed by the liturgical choreography and the latter will be so impacted by our embodied preaching that the sermon will swirl around the baptism, or the prayers of the people, or the sharing of peace will find its home in such immediate vicinity of the sermon that the idea of good fencing making good neighbors will simply not apply.[6]

No such dramatic transformations of the worship event may occur at all. We may instead experience only a quiet growth of integrity between sermon and other worship elements that increasingly strengthens congregations in gospel reality and empowers them as individual members and as a whole body to live out gospel more and more in all that they do and everywhere they go. Preaching as gospel aims at empowering people to experience and embrace the freedom that gospel provides us to be who we are meant to be: fully embodied, integrated, whole participants in loving, dialogical relationship choreographed by God.

Long-term Possibilities

This kind of preaching/worship enterprise may redesign Christian life. When gospel enlivens us wholly, when gospel claims us in our DNA and in our ligaments, in our olfactory sense and our nerve endings, and not just in our ears, a lot of the rules defined by various traditions and habits, theological or otherwise, begin to change or even to evaporate as gospel designs our individual lives and our lives together around new patterns, processes, and movements. This can happen because gospel is itself not static, but dynamic, and therefore our relationship with God,

---

[5] See chapter 15 as an example.

[6] Robert Frost, "Mending Wall." "Something there is that doesn't love a wall, That sends the frozen ground swell under it, And spills the upper boulders in the sun; And makes gaps even two can pass abreast." And again, "Before I built a wall I'd ask to know What I was walling in or walling out, And to whom I was like to give offense. Something there is that doesn't love a wall, That wants it down." Oscar Williams and Edwin Honig, eds., *The Mentor Book of Major American Poets* (New York and Scarborough, Ontario: The New American Library, 1962), 235–36.

each other, and the whole creation is always, if only subtly, on the move. If we are faithful to it, gospel will not permit us long to rest on our status quos, for we are ever beckoned/whirled by the Spirit into new ways of being, doing, relating, even as we are confronted by our global ecosystem to adjust and adapt to the new realities it daily sets before us.

Yet some things we trust will never change. The love of God for us, God's loving presence with us, and our absolute dependence on both of those realities will remain the ground and center of our whole being. What changes is how we embody that for ourselves and so for others of a Sunday morning, in the library or at the supermarket, amidst terrible famines in Africa, in the face of plagues like breast cancer or AIDS, as a counter to domestic and global violence and warfare. Such preaching is probably not a miracle cure for our past or present failures in authentically living gospel. But it can move us toward wholeness, because it honors the whole reality God so deeply loves.

PART III

Contexts

CHAPTER 6

Time and the "Christian Year"

What do we know about time? We speak of quantitative time, *chronos*, and experience it as linear time as history marches us from the past into the future. We also know *chronos* as circular, with daily, monthly, yearly rhythms moving us from yesterday to tomorrow. We talk about time in relationship to us, as an external "given" to us: at birth, we may receive hours, months, or years of life as a gift. How much time will you give me to finish this task, make up my mind, pay off my mortgage? If we commit a crime we may be given time in jail. We experience chronological time internally in the beat of our hearts and the time it takes for a pinprick to manifest itself in the brain as "ouch!" We know time as a valuer, measuring the worth of work and family by it. For heaven's sake, don't waste my time!

Time can be uncanny, slippery stuff. Even though the past is past, many of us have discovered ourselves in reverie, mysteriously "relocated" in moments of memory. We know, too, the peculiar feeling of *déjà vu* or a sense of the future now. Science fiction enthusiasts talk about time warps, but Christians are more likely to describe unexpected rearrangements of time and history as *xairos*, God's time.

Xairos is unconventional time, interrupting and changing forever chronological human time. *Xairos* rests at the heart of the notion of *anamnesis*—the idea that in the Sabbath Seder the Jewish family "recovers" the sense of being present in the original Passover moment or a Christian at the cross. "Were you there when they crucified my Lord?" [*sic*] the old hymn asks. Who has sung that and never experienced a sense of being somehow present on that hill of horror? *Xairos* also bespeaks the future present, or realized eschatology. To the degree that we feast at the heavenly table here and now, that we are able to work even small miracles of love, that we can shift the balance of the world even a fraction toward life manifests the in-breaking of God's completion of promises into our un-likely present. Or so the classic theology of time goes.

Time, however we view it, presents us with a theological issue. What does living in loving, dialogical relationship with God and neighbor have to say about our relationship with and in time? Time *is* the context in which God relates with us. Jesus of Nazareth lived in specific years, yet God engages with us in *our* particular time. Time *is* the construct within which humans engage in relational activity: we can be together lovingly or unlovingly in time, but we cannot, insofar as we know, be together outside of time when we, in fact, live in time.

Marking Time?

Until a couple of decades ago, many Protestants never thought much about time as a fundamental construct of worship. We didn't want to be late for church, of course, and we wanted to get home afterward in time to get dinner out of the oven. Christmas and Easter came around regu-larly—well, Christmas at least was always dependable, even if Easter never seemed to settle down to a steady date. Since Vatican II, however, we have experienced increasing interest in and emphasis on observing the "litur-gical year" or "Christian year" as a fixed pattern of special and ordinary days. Now most denominations use a lectionary that provides each day with selected biblical texts and defines special seasons complete with des-ignated themes and colors. Is it an "ordinary" Sunday? Preachers and presiders will wear something green. And well you may ask why, since the adoption of particular colors for particular days probably has more to do with socio-economic reality than with theology!

We *can* identify many good reasons for interest in and emphasis on this "Christian year." In the first place, the designated calendar and lectionary remind us that God involves the divine self in human lives *over time* and calls us to consider time as a *theological* constant in the ordering of our daily life. Given the increasing demands of secular society to attend to its claims, such a reminder can be comforting for Christians. Indeed, some understand the "liturgical year" with its lectionary primarily as the way the church marks time. Calendars with dates marked in fixed colors and listing specified biblical readings can provide Christians disoriented by the increasing pluralism of society with a clear road map through the year. By attending to that calendar we can discern to some degree where Chris-tians are on the time journey, and we can perhaps mark our progress.[1]

---

[1] Susan Roll has recently presented a paper on this notion of the journey as a model for the pattern of celebrating festal time. Susan K. Roll, "Beyond Dualistic Models of Festal

And yet, we do not share a singular experience of time. At any moment, I may experience time moving at the speed of light or in slow motion, while others have it ambling along at their own comfortable pace. Some people love the dawn hours, others the deep dark of night, still others mid-afternoon. In order to facilitate relationship within diversity humans do try to manage time, to get it under control so we all operate on the same time—or at least within consistent time zone patterns! Calendars, clocks, flight schedules, reminders about due-dates all attest to our efforts to control the subjectivity of time. How could we live without these?

Still, does anyone really love their alarm clock? rush hour? the design of the academic term? Like many Northeners living with seasonal affective disorder, I am wholly dysfunctional at Midnight Christmas Eve services and Easter Sunrise services. And what of those who must work on Sunday? If you do not struggle with your own internal clock's disjunction with other's expectations, are you comfortable with a secular chronology increasingly insensitive to that of the "Church Year?" How well do we deal with a Christmas season that starts in the malls with Halloween but in the church on December 25? For many in the north, at least, winter doldrums need to be evaporated by frivolity and levity just when the church is sobering us through Lent, having quite forgotten that Sundays celebrate resurrection and therefor offer us every reason to feast! Such conflicts leave many people ill at ease.[2]

Meanwhile, the movement of the calendar does recognize primal human rhythms of ebb and flow, including our need for marking anniversaries and passages and our need for stability and change. These are important considerations. But can faith experience, the experience of loving God-with-us, be expressed by or regulated by *quantitative* instruments? Is the "Christian year" really a matter of this kind of time? That the church participates in such an exercise of chronos, of timekeeping by maintaining a fixed liturgical year, may in fact manifest a surrender to a lifestyle antithetical to gospel.

Historicism

Some view the "liturgical year" as the means by which we celebrate "historical" events, ideas, or persons, thereby commemorating and even attempting to reexperience past encounters with God. In aid of this, the

Time," presented at the Congress "Lichamelijkheid, religie en gender," Fontana Nieuweschans Landelijk Onderzoeksprogramma, Nederland, December, 1997.

[2]There is a longstanding tradition of the fourth Sunday of Lent dispensing with the Lenten purples for the joyful pinks of spring, probably because the people refused to give up their festal celebration of the spring equinox!

whole Christian year appears to attempt the reconstruction of a "life of Jesus" so that we can "walk the roads of Palestine with Jesus." Of course, scriptures do not give us a chronology of Jesus' life; rather, each gospel writer has his own to offer. Moreover, the determination of dates for such events as Jesus' birth and death may have had more to do with cultural, political, sociological, and perhaps whimsical factors than historical "truth" or even theology did. We address them best as symbols, but even then need to ask if they are coherent with our turn-of-the-century realities.

Moreover, a friend and colleague takes exception with the notion that we can possibly "remember" what we didn't witness—be it the birth of Jesus or the conversion of Paul. He has a point. Feminist scholarship has often taken a different slant, seeking to remember, reconstruct, women's stories that have been written out of history. But can we take the bits and pieces of scriptural and extracanonical witness and put together an "event-that-was?" Even if we could, can celebrating Pentecost as an *historical* occasion even begin to do justice to the working of God's Spirit in the past or enable us to experience the activity of the Spirit in our own lives? While sitting through another of those Christmas bathrobe dramas and remembering my own experiences of participating in them, I often wonder how many children suffer through them without ever getting even a taste of the extraordinary love of God expressed in the words and deeds of Jesus. Perhaps the weight put on events, persons, and abstract ideas of the *past* makes occasional, nominal, theoretical Christians instead of year-round and actual ones.

True, history can beckon us to and aid us in attending to the roots that partly fund our identity and help map out directions for our future. Thus part of the task of all Christians is to carry on the community memories and interpretation of memories. Still, we need to ask how often the "year" succeeds in expressing the historical content but not the essence of gospel. How well does it provide for the possibility of experiencing God's loving involvement with us now, of empowering our relationships now, and *not* necessarily in the same ways we claim God to have been involved with individuals and communities in the past?

Theological Claims or Experience of Gospel?

Everything we do makes a theological claim of one kind or another; everything we do attests and enables life, or undergirds death. What theological statements do our celebrations of the "Christian year" make? For example, most churches celebrate Christmas with extravagance, while many pews remain empty on Sundays, and even Easter often pales in comparison to Christmas splendor. This portrays Christmas as the most important day of the year, but is it? Many claim Sunday, the celebration of resurrection, as the fundamental feast of the Christian community. What speaks loudest?

Or consider this. For all I know of the historical and theological foundations of placing ashes on foreheads in an Ash Wednesday service, ashes continue to speak most loudly to me of the deadly residue of cancerous cigarettes, the messy dregs of a cozy winter fire, and the devastating remains of forest conflagrations. I am not at all convinced that ash-crossed foreheads at the beginning of Lent really represent lives in transformation toward loving one's disliked neighbors. We might ask as well of the value of Christ candles and Advent wreaths in a technological society such as ours. Does such frail light suffice to push back the dark and adequately portray the extraordinary brilliance of the One who illuminates us? Perhaps it does somewhere, but in winter in Canada we are dependent on much more powerful light for healthy living. And what of such "theme feasts" as Trinity Sunday? For all the systematic theologies that come forth from pulpits then, I am not at all convinced celebrating this day makes better Christians!

The violence and horror of sexism and heterosexism, racism and ageism, of fear-laden expansion of economic disparity, and the cosmic pollution of our earth home at least partially frame the context in which gospel challenges us to expand our limited concepts of God and consider what it means to be loved by and in life-giving relationship with God and God's family. Given the varied degree and effectiveness with which churches address these realities begs us to ask if the "year" creatively participates in this process of gospel happening in our reality. Or does it reinforce what is, in fact, antithetical to gospel? Some women, for example, find much of the "year" a patriarchal construct exclusive of and inimical to women's wholeness.[3] It is harder to know how the "year" influenced or failed to end the conflict in Ireland or addresses the relentless poverty in two-thirds of the world's countries. True, the calendar's cyclical nature gives us opportunity to recognize that with God a fresh start in the face of our failures is always a welcome option. Yet throughout the seasons of the "Christian year," as we attend to the expectations of set days and emphases, welfare recipients can only afford a diet guaranteed to ruin their health,

---

[3]See, e.g., Ann Patrick Ware, "The Easter Vigil: A Theological and Liturgical Critique," in *Women at Worship: Interpretations of North American Diversity*, ed. Marjorie Procter-Smith and Janet R. Walton (Louisville: Westminster/John Knox Press, 1993). Ware notes that the Easter Vigil is dualistic, full of phallic symbols, male language, hierarchy, neglects social and cosmic ills and issues, endorses congregational passivity, etc. Even where the vigil is not celebrated, much of what the liturgical year highlights readily falls under the same critique.

infants and grandparents are bludgeoned to death by their next of kin, indigenous people continue to be prohibited from full participation in life, and threats and violence continue to be seen as an acceptable means of ending conflict and controlling others. I wonder for how many the six Sundays of Lent or veiling the cross truly empower protest of the endless crucifixions that go on daily in our own house and around the world. The questions and the answers are both crucial and difficult. Perhaps we would do better to construct years around loving one's enemies, creating a just society, healing the earth, and caring faithfully for one's dependents.

Lectionary

Using a common lectionary can help diverse congregations experience a sense of identity with the whole body of Christ through addressing the same biblical texts of a Sunday and within the same calendrical context. It offers access to the words and deeds of Jesus from the five different major theological perspectives of the writers of Matthew, Mark, Luke, John, and Paul. Moreover, the lectionary can challenge preachers who might otherwise fall into the habit of preaching on only a few favorite passages with new sermon texts so that congregations have the hope of encountering an astonishing richness and diversity of expressions of experience with God and gospel. At the same time, a common lectionary provides for the possibility of extensive planning well in advance, inviting congregational involvement in sermon and worship preparation, the harmonizing of music and other arts with scripture, the nourishing of ecumenical conversations, and the generation of useful resources for study. The lectionary clearly has potential for generating gospel relationship.

Yet too rarely do we experience preaching from texts other than those of Matthew, Mark, and Luke. In a preaching class one year, my students were astonished to experience the Older Testament Deborah as a metaphor for—embodier of—God. But I have never been ready to admit that gospel is not found there, that Ezra and Obadiah have no gospel to offer, or that psalms are not proper texts for preaching. The Pauline letters, Paul Scott Wilson has suggested, were preached.[4] And why should not Leah, Benjamin, or Dorcas be permitted to tell their own gospel stories?

Too often, as well, biblical texts appear in worship on a lectionary's recommendation without anyone giving due care to their context, without thinking through who now might be hurt or confused by them.

---

[4] Paul S. Wilson, "Paul's Letters: A Homiletical Perspective," *Toronto Journal of Theology* 11/1 (Spring 1995): 59–69.

Careless use of stories of violence against the "other," of texts expressing Paul's misogyny, of verses filled with anti-Jewish polemic stop gospel cold. So also can allowing the lectionary to silence those who desperately need to have the authenticity of their relationship with God brought to speech. Lectionaries leave out a lot of scripture and questions regarding whose theological agenda governs the making of choices need to be asked.[5] Certainly too strict observance of lectionary expectations impoverishes us.[6]

Calvin preached *lectio continua*, straight through whole books of scripture, expecting to find gospel everywhere in the Bible. Perhaps he was right to do so, and he was certainly wise in being *open* to finding gospel anywhere. But many, on the basis of experience or the horror stories of others believe there are unreadable, unpreachable texts, texts which so violate "others" that they should not now be addressed in public precisely because they do not manifest gospel. Even if all texts are valid in theory, we must think twice about burdening the preacher and or congregation with texts that one or the other cannot handle. Perhaps the same should be said about the various parts of the "Christian year."

Both of these constructs, lectionary and year, ought to give us pause. In my view, we have uncritically assumed ancient patterns, ideas, symbols to be normative for all time, leaving many assumptions, theological and otherwise, unchallenged. How much of what we have appropriated is incoherent with gospel either in the first place, or because it simply does not speak to our time and our realities? How much that is important in our lives is being ignored?

Authenticity

Luther's test of authenticity—whether or not Christ is preached— remains a useful measure for us. Does the "year," inclusive of its feast days and its lectionary, proclaim Christ? Does *all* of it proclaim Christ? Does it proclaim *all* of Christ? In the terms of this volume, we might better ask if and how well the "year" and lectionary facilitate loving, dialogical relationship with God and neighbor in this worship event amid our realities? Or do we need other means to help relationship with God to happen?

---

[5]Eugene Lowry makes the point that liturgists, not preachers, have traditionally created lectionaries, thus nuancing them in the direction of liturgical rather than homiletical interests. Eugene L. Lowry, *Living with the Lectionary: Preaching Through the Revised Common Lectionary* (Nashville: Abingdon Press, 1992).

[6] Lowry notes also that "in the last decade of increased mainline Protestant use of the common lectionary, sermons—on average—have become more biblical, more boring, and less evocative." *The Sermon,* 41.

If we perceive and celebrate the "year" as timekeeping for the purpose of inducing *xairos*, or as a mechanism for commemorative focus on historical persons, events, doctrines, or alternately, if we abandon any coherent plan of scriptural address, we risk separating ourselves from gospel. Gospel ultimately has to do *not* with time keeping, with past events or doctrine, or even with faith as object or substance. It has rather to do with ongoing, unfolding, deepening encounter between humankind and gracious God over time. Gospel is the reality and process of being embraced in life-giving, loving relationship with God and neighbor; gospel *is* relationship. We cannot function out of an orientation to the past; we cannot live out of a purely conceptual consideration of gospel as proclaimed in history[7] or anticipated in an eventual future. When we are thirsty we need water: not the memory of it, not the promise of it, but water—cool, wet, thirst-quenching water. Grain will not grow on the memory or the promise of it and neither will we.

God's love *has* been experienced by people in the past in ways attested to by scripture and particularly and definitively by the words and deeds of Jesus of Nazareth. Jesus did, we believe, quench the thirst of the woman at the well and the partygoers at Cana. These biblical witnesses are essential for us because they claim the continuity of loving relationship and inform our present and future reality. But we do not re-experience or remember those events of God's love, *we experience God's love directly in our time and amid our realities.*

Shifting Perspectives

We need history to help keep us constantly connected with gracious God amid the chaos of our ever-changing world, so that we are always surrounded by and suffused with God's loving presence and thereby enabled to embody that gift to and for the world. But the task of the church is not finally to recall or commemorate history. Because we are not the same as we were yesterday, patterns which used to be appropriate may no longer be. We dare not assume that the "Christian year" and the lectionary as we know them suit the interchange of gospel and twenty-first century Christians in a wide diversity of geographical, social, and political contexts.

We might rather begin to think of these as flexible resources for gospel happening for us, here, now, asking of them specific questions about how a particular event or season, theme or color enables or enhances our

---

[7]Calvin does speak of "remembering" our baptism (*Institutes,* 4.15.3) and speaks of the supper as a memorial and remembrancer [*sic*] (*Institutes,* 4.18.6). But his argument clearly attests that in each case we claim the present reality of God with us.

dialogical life of love. We might pair each year's readings with a contemporary issue—economic disparity local and global, constitutional crises, congregational conflict or celebration. We might, as I suggested earlier, regularly create new lectionaries around such ever-changing issues. In any case, the point is not to make either a constructed chronology of Jesus' life or the particular contemporary reality the focus, but to keep gospel in conversation with us as we struggle to live as faithful Christians committed to bodying forth life in the world.

That might mean, of course, spending Christmas eve in a women's shelter with women and children who, unlike Mary, have been abandoned or persecuted by husbands and fathers. That might mean working with them not just through six weeks of Lent, but until they truly experience new life after the death of a fundamental relationship and postponing Easter until all are ready to celebrate resurrection. Or perhaps it will mean celebrating Easter in February, because that is when we northerners are most likely depressed and weighed down and hopeless, and what must that be like if one also lives in a shelter? The possibilities abound. We need only to release ourselves from imposed expectations and let our imaginations be powered by the Spirit who seeks to create a new earth out of the old one.

We do struggle to live faithfully in relationship with God who is present with us and for us constantly—but not necessarily in ways historically described or even in historically identifiable acts. Our job is to find ways to help one another embody the gospel proclaimed in scripture, so that gospel can enliven all the world. It is to focus on and encourage the event of gospel in the whole of worship; to generate, sustain, enhance life-giving relationship between God and God's people in this time and this place. Surely we can do this!

CHAPTER 7

Pastoral Reality

I learned at a very young age that the "proper" attitude before God was awe, reverence, and fear. I was allowed only to be quiet in the sanctuary, whether anything was going on or not. We whispered, tiptoed, and never, never ran in the sanctuary. The sanctuary was a "holy" place, where only "holy" people were permitted, quiet, respectful, properly behaved people. But I learned also that Jesus said "let the little children come to me, for of such is the economy of God." Now the little children I knew were *not* quiet—except when sick or sleeping—and certainly none was holy, perfectly well-behaved and whatever other impossible things "holy" meant. Being a child was playing and laughing and jumping up and down with excitement and crying when we were hurt or worn out—but never in church, how odd.

I was taught, too, that God is love. I couldn't quite figure out what love had to do with awe, reverence, and fear. I knew what fear was—it was being terrified (at age three) that my parents had abandoned me forever when they left me with my stranger-aunt while they boarded a boat and sailed off to Catalina Island. Fear was running away from strangers who offered you candy and going paralyzed at the threats of the bullies at school. I wasn't too sure about awe and reverence, but I knew what fear was. I *didn't* know what it had to do with God-is-love. I did know what love is—hugs and being tucked into bed at night and my parents coming back from Catalina Island after all.

Things got more complicated as I grew up and discovered sometimes that I was downright angry with God, and if God sees into our hearts and knows everything, what was I supposed to do—pretend I wasn't angry and sing the happy hymn anyway? Even if we couldn't spell it, we all knew by age eight what a hypocrite was. Later, as a teenager, like every

71

other teenager, I was just confused and wasn't at all sure I believed in God in the first place. Still, I was expected to recite the creeds as if nothing were wrong. Eventually, when I fell in love it was a good thing nobody asked me to be awed, reverent, and fearful—because my cup was flowing over with exuberance and ecstasy, and it was about time, thank you kindly. But when in spite of all my efforts, my marriage died, I began to wonder whatever happened to lament—because that was all I had in me some days, all I was capable of, no matter how hard I tried.

The reality of our lives shapes us and, for better or worse, shapes our engagement in worship events. But how often does a worship event of a Sunday or those over a course of Sundays take seriously the wildly diverse affective states of those who gather? Too often, I suspect, an unconscious or conscious assumption expects we will put all that on hold, leave it outside the sanctuary doors, stow it under the pew while we pay attention (!) to what happens in the worship event. Worship events commonly address us not only as a homogenized crowd, but also as an affectless one. When worship events ignore our emotional realities the events easily blur as well into a gray sameness. But if God addresses us as whole persons, if the Spirit of Indwelling Presence lives with us through the entirety of our living, something in this picture looks quite out of focus.

What the Psalms Tell Us

The book of Psalms offers a different view, that of the Hebrew people-in-conversation-with-God, in relationship with God and neighbor. And what a vibrant mosaic of conversation it is! Yes, there are psalms that express the awe and reverence expected of me as a child—for example Psalm 8.[1]

"Oh God, our Sovereign, how majestic is your name in all the earth! You have set your glory above the heavens. Out of the mouth of babes and infants, you have founded a bulwark because of your foes, to silence the enemy and the avenger. When I look at the heavens, the work of your fingers, the moon and the stars which you have established; what are human beings that you are mindful of them, mortals that you care for them? Yet you have made them a little lower than God, and crowned them with glory and honour. You have given them dominion over the works of your hands.... Oh God, our sovereign, how majestic is your name in all the earth!"

---

[1] All psalms are from *The New Testament and Psalms: An Inclusive Version* (New York, Oxford: Oxford University Press, 1995). See also 19, 84.

Who would quarrel that this presents a potent, viable, and essential honoring of God-in-relationship with us? Neither, I think, would any of us disagree with its affective character of awe and profound joy. Similarly, psalms that praise, thank, and delight in God constitute a fundamental part of our life with God. Blessed continually with God's creative and sustaining love, how could we fail to live our lives thankfully? So Psalm 92 begins:

> It is good to give thanks to God, to sing praises to your name, O Most High; to declare your steadfast love in the morning, and your faithfulness at night, to the music of the lute and the harp, to the melody of the lyre. For you, O God, have made me glad by your work; at the works of your hands I sing for joy.

And how many psalms carry the refrain, "Oh give thanks to God for God is good, for God's steadfast love endures forever?"[2] Nor is this praise of God quiet, for we are called to clap our hands, shout, to sing, to make a joyful noise with trumpets and other subtle, unimpassioned instruments![3] According to these texts, many of us are much too quiet, much too somber in our worship gatherings!

Of course, there are quiet psalms, psalms of reverence, affirmation, and comfort, like Psalm 23: "God is my shepherd, I shall not want," and Psalm 121: "If I lift up my eyes to the hills, from where will my help come?" Akin to these are psalms of love, like Psalm 18:

> I love you, O God, my strength. God is my rock, my fortress and my deliverer, my God, my rock, in whom I take refuge, my shield, and the horn of my salvation, my stronghold. I call upon God who is worthy to be praised, so I shall be saved from my enemies.

This language and affect resonate well with most Christians, but not all the psalms address God in such a "positive" or pleasant way. Note, for example, the psalms of abandonment, confusion, and despair, like Psalm 22:

> My God, my God, why have you forsaken me? Why are you so far from helping me, from the words of my groaning? O my God, I cry by day, but you do not answer...I am poured out like water, and all my bones are out of joint; my heart is like wax, it is melted within my breast; my mouth is dried up like a potsherd, and my tongue sticks to my jaws; you lay me in the dust of death.

---

[2] Psalm 136:1; Psalm 118; see also Psalm 9; 34; etc.
[3] Psalm 47; 81; 96; 98; 147—150.

Such a text reads easily off a page like this one, but when we recover the sense most of us have experienced at one time or another of God's absence in our lives, when we remember that this psalm has been attributed to Jesus as he hung dying on the cross, we begin to touch anew the frightening, swirling, swallowing-up abyss of being absolutely cut off from love. Such a psalm cries out to be read aloud, on one's feet. Similarly, Psalm 88 cries out for embodied discovery: "O God, why do you cast me off? Why do you hide your face from me?" Perhaps, if the terror of such alienation haunts us too much, such psalms can only be whispered.

Psalms of lament like the "how long" psalms can push us even farther into the affective potency of Hebrew life with God. The psalms of anger and demand may surprise us by their very presence in scripture, they may shock us by their vehemence:

> Vindicate me, O God, for *I* have walked in my integrity, I have trusted in God *without wavering*. Prove me, O God, and try me, test my heart and my mind...*I* do not sit with the worthless, nor do I consort with hypocrites; I *hate* the company of evildoers, and *will not sit* with the wicked. I wash my hands in *innocence...*[4]

This psalmist is clearly furious with the Holy One, as is the author of Psalm 44, as s/he shouts: "Rouse yourself! Why do you sleep, O God? Awake, do not cast us off forever...Rise up, come to our help."[5] In truth, few of us never grow angry with God. I suspect many of us vent that anger in private or simmer under the visible surface of Sunday morning docility. Nor are such experiences confined to individuals, yet how many congregations even acknowledge such reality, let alone address it in a worship event? Even if we as individuals or as a congregation have frequently screamed these words with our internal voices, if the words even appear in worship we likely voice them in a manner that touches none of the reality they enfold. How easily we come under the judgment of the apocalypticist: "because you are lukewarm, and neither cold nor hot, I am about to spit you out of my mouth" (Revelation 3:16).

Confession and surrender may be the closest we come to claiming our inner angst. Most of us would find confession appropriate especially after an outburst like those above, although that surely was not the motive behind psalms like 51:

---

[4] Psalm 26, emphasis mine.
[5] See also Psalm 35; 69; 141; 142; 7; 17.

Have mercy on me, O God...for I know my transgressions, and my sin is ever before me. Against you, you only, have I sinned, and done what is evil in your sight...

We may find it easy, also, to express the restless hunger of the psalms of waiting and longing for God: "I wait for God, my soul waits and in God's word I hope; my soul waits for God more than those who watch for the morning..."[6] and, "O God, you are my God, I long for you from early morning; my whole being desires you, like a dry, worn out and water-less land my soul is thirsty for you."[7]

I do wonder, though, in spite of the frequency of use of psalms of trust and confidence, if we really experience the assurance they offer: "God is our refuge and strength, a very present help in trouble. Therefore we will not fear though the earth should change, though the mountains shake..."[8] Do we really believe this? Does the expression of these words, the embodiment of them in worship truly show their power in our lives? Perhaps their authenticity lies more in the deeper prayer of the unbeliever who fears very much indeed and prays the psalm seeking the reassurance she or he doesn't feel.

These psalm fragments even taken out of context offer real impetus for broadening the affective horizons of any congregation, for they reflect a full range of human mood and emotion from agony to ecstasy,[9] and a full range of volume, from whispers to clanging cymbals. Why should they not? If we agree that worship is life lived out in loving, dialogical relationship with God and God's global family, if we agree that God loves us as whole persons and lives with us in all our human experiences, even to the pain and anguish of death, then we will admit that all our moods and emotions belong part and parcel to authentic relationship, and thus worship. Not only are they admissible, but essential.

Are we overflowing with ecstatic love for God? Overwhelmed with gratefulness? We are pretty clear about our expectation that worship events will include these affections of the heart, although we will not likely dance them there, to our great loss. But what if we are angry with God? hurt? confused about God (to say nothing about our relationship with our neighbor!)? Honest relationship with God and neighbor demands

---

[6]Psalm 130; see also 62, etc.

[7]Psalm 63, eds. John Allyn Melloh, S.M., and William G. Storey, *Praise God in Song: Ecumenical Daily Prayer* (Chicago: GIA Publications, Inc., 1979), 42. The editors attribute the translation to the *Good News Bible*—Old Testament, American Bible Society, 1976. See also Psalm 42.

[8]Psalm 46.

[9]Including laughter, Ps. 126.

honest expression of mood and feeling in all our worship. Because love does. Love is what worship is all about, after all: loving dialogical relationship with God and neighbor, authentic caring about and for one another.

The Hospitable Inclusivity of Gospel

Gospel embraces us with love, invites us to care for one another, and frees us to be authentically human. Gospel names us as beloved not as perfect, holy people but as people who are filled with a crazy-quilt of emotions and affections rooted in a vast matrix of realities. Gospel also identifies us as people who struggle continuously to be both honest and caring. Part of our responsibility in worship events, then, is to enable each other to relate with God and one another authentically. That means worship events need to address pain as well as joy, confusion as well as clarity, anger as well as delight, honestly and openly and in regard to God and one another. Invitations and encouragement to express honestly our reality, well-crafted words arising out of lived, felt experience, dynamism in tone of voice and gesture all can begin the process of releasing one another into the freedom of weeping, dancing, whispering, laughing our true life with God and each other in worship events.

Such freedom makes room for those who cannot be joyful just because the church happens to be celebrating Christmas right now, for those for whom resurrection occurs in the middle of Lent, for those who cannot recite the words of any creed because they are too confused about what that faith is or because the words fail them. Loving, dialogical relationship makes room for mourners to weep and the homeless and jobless to lament; it invites us to help the confused and the angry to struggle through their reality so they can come to reconciliation and peace. Would we not manage this at the family reunion, where some may come having just buried a child and some bursting with the joy of a new partnership? Why, then, not in worship where the diversity of reality spans just as much?

We honor the diversity of needs within a congregation first and foremost by embodying gospel—that God comes to us in our reality, whatever that happens to be this day, and offers the divine Self to us in love. We pastorally care for others in worship when we pray for those who are sick or lonely or entering into new relationships or a reconfigured life, when we keep one another close to our hearts and minds, and when we are as involved as possible in the process of developing sermons and whole worship events. Perhaps instead of simply asking for announcements we could ask rather if anyone has a joy to celebrate, a woe to lament, a puzzle needing solving, or a task wanting support. Surely, if this worship event truly manifests living, dialogical relationship, we can learn how to read in one another's faces and postures what may not be spoken and how to be present with one another in ways beyond the customary expectations of Sunday morning behavior. We know how to do this—we do it all the time at home and at work. We have let all those notions of "proper" and "correct" behaviour in church all too often stifle the same tender, loving care in church. Gospel can and does release us!

Because worship involves whole human beings it deals with affect and emotion, it embraces the physical as fully as the inseparable spiritual. Thus, a worship event has the capacity to heal, comfort, enliven if it is authentic worship, worship that enables healthy relationship with God and God's global community. Nor do I mean to suggest that worship events function as group therapy, or as a free-for-all of passion without any restraint of or responsibility for our feelings or what we do with them. Honest relationship—loving, dialogical relationship—does call for accountability, responsibility, caring for the neighbor as much as we care for ourselves. We are, after all, about the business of giving life, and part of that process is enabling others to be who they are so that healing can occur, so that joy can be experienced, so that love can be shed abroad in the world.

Beyond Affect

We cannot define pastoral realities solely in terms of affect, of course. We need also honor other realities by providing wheelchair access for those who are so mobilized, signing for those who perceive through senses other than the ears, good lighting and large-print text so all can easily see to read. We need as well to find ways of empowering the participation of those who do not read by more frequently lining out hymns[10] and prayers. We can use smoke-free candles and avoid incense unless we are certain no one, not even the unexpected visitor, suffers from asthma or other respiratory difficulties. Empowering people to choose freely whether or not to participate in certain dimensions of the service—a hymn, the communion, kneeling or standing, sharing the peace—on the basis of theology or physiology or emotional need or other personal condition makes up another essential step of the practice of such hospitality.[11]

---

[10]This has been common where hymnbooks are not readily available. The practice is simple: A song leader sings one line, and the congregation sings it back. The leader sings the next line, and the congregation repeats it, and so on to the end. This provides a useful way of assisting congregations in learning new hymns as well.

[11] Although focused on preaching, valuable help in understanding and responding to the realities of persons with disabilities can be found in Kathy Black, *A Healing Homiletic: Preaching and Disability* (Nashville: Abingdon Press, 1996).

Worship as living in loving, dialogical relationship with God and neighbor means assurance of hospitality to all who come to a worship event regardless of the state in which they come; it means finding ways of honoring a range of emotional, intellectual, physical conditions, of being intentionally inclusive and caring of all persons in whatever their life-situation. God relates with us in all the fullness of our particular and ever-changing realities, and invites us to embody that in all our circumstances, including—especially including—our worship events.

Congregational Identity[12]

Still, worship is not the pursuit of singular individuals. A community is more than an aggregation of beings. In our faith journey we interconnect and weave together with brothers and sisters in the pew, in the street, around the world. So we need attend not only to individual diversity and reality when thinking about, designing, and implementing worship events. We need also to attend to unique congregational identity, reality, mood, need.

Faith communities are not all alike, and the disparities may be just as great between one tall-steeple, "fat and sassy" city congregation and another in the same metropolis as they are between such a community and the most "impoverished," deep-in-the-hills, or urban ghetto congregation we can find. At the same time, there may be much in common between many, perhaps most, congregations, and perhaps we might one day discover a kind of lowest-common-denominator choreography that would embody universally the essence of Christian community. But even if we did, I am not at all convinced it would do us much good. Congregations, for all they may look alike, are just not the same.[13] We may not remember this often enough, however, nor that last Sunday's gathering at Kirk-by-the-River Church is not the same as this Sunday's or next week's assembly in the same place. What happens to the congregation as a whole as well as in part can radically alter its sense of identity or mood as quickly as these can change for an individual—and it does not necessarily require the sanctuary to go up in fire and smoke or a pillar of the community to die for this to occur.

---

[12]The following rehearses material originally published in Pamela Ann Moeller, *A Kinesthetic Homiletic: Embodying Gospel in Preaching* (Minneapolis: Fortress Press, 1993), chap. 5.

[13]Some useful volumes addressing the dimensions shaping congregations differently include: James F. Hopewell, *Congregation: Stories and Structure* (Philadelphia: Fortress Press, 1987); Arthur Van Seters, ed., *Preaching as a Social Act: Theology and Practice* (Nashville: Abingdon Press, 1988); and John S. McClure, *The Four Codes of Preaching: Rhetorical Strategies* (Minneapolis: Fortress Press, 1991).

That means that with every Sunday's planning, the question needs to be asked again: Where is this people now? Because the process is a corporate one, the pastor's assessment is not enough. Indeed, the more members of the community that actively work through the process, the more likely multiple dimensions of current reality will be responsibly identified. The worship planning group may then choose to focus on one text, style of prayer, or hymn over the other because the first meets this people where they are better than that one does. How else can we be reasonably sure of connecting this gospel with the whole of who these people are?

Congregational identity does not grow in a vacuum, of course. Every congregation lives within a larger context of community, geography, climate, culture(s), politics; and every congregation lives within the context of a global village filled to the brim with diversity, change, life, and death. As individuals and as congregations, we participate in an incredible ecosystem that affects what we say, do, and are, and that we affect in return. If we find our world hostile to the poor or to folk of a particular ethnicity, how might that transform our embodiment of gospel by way of vision or impetus for living out this day's faith relationships? "Little children, love one another." How can we do this when the world surrounding us is more than happy to eat us alive, to run us down and leave us but a shadow on the pavement, all without even noticing? How can we hand out paper bulletins by the fistful on Sunday without considering the ancient redwood forests of the Northwest or the Brazilian rainforests? What of our global pastoral reality influences or can be influenced by our embodiment of gospel this day? What does our world need of us this Sunday? What shall we do to bring it life, to provide it with the worshipful pastoral care we all require within our dialogical relationship with God and all God's creation?

Moods, realities, needs, pastoral care are all of a piece, interwoven dimensions of loving, dialogical relationship with God and neighbor. Attending to them in worship events is not about catering to anyone, about consumerism, about worship being defined by human need. Honoring the full scope of human and global reality in worship events belongs to the Christian project of being faithful companions with God through being faithful companions with each other. It is about affirming freedoms—freedom not to sing a hymn that does not this day belong to you, freedom not to recite a creed or prayer response if it seems incoherent babble or destructive drivel, freedom to dance in the aisles or take a real chunk of bread instead of a pinch, freedom to choose life-giving cultural symbols to express gospel instead of those imposed by missionary imperialism, freedom to make mistakes and to experience gospel in places/persons/activities we could never have imagined might embody them. And always it is freedom in relation with those whom God calls us to love as much as ourselves such that we may all come to be who we are meant to be: fully embodied, integrated, whole participants in the loving, graceful choreography of God. How can we best honor gospel freedom this day, in this reality?

CHAPTER 8

Special Occasions

There have been days in my life when I haven't paid much attention to God and days when I hope God isn't paying much attention to me. However, if God truly is the source of our being, if God is incarnational and dwells in us, even my least appealing moments are very much part of God's engagement with me. Given that God relates with us as whole persons and remains with us through all our life-experiences, we can properly address all of life in worship events. My days of faithlessness and even tediousness I would rather not make much of in this way, although precisely those are part and parcel of Sunday-by-Sunday worshipfare. Indeed, we have consistently claimed God embraces us and engages with us exactly when we are least lovable. I find it difficult to comprehend such love, particularly when we humans are muddling along in utter dullness. Rebellion at least offers a challenge, but tedium? That God puts up with such never fails to amaze me and to expand my appreciation of the extraordinary capacity of God to continually exceed our expectations.

All our days are not ordinary days, at least in our very subjective view. Occasions and events that can generate a spectrum of feeling and behavior from profound anguish to ecstatic joy punctuate our lives, roust us out of our habitual patterns, and stir up in us a hunger to connect in a special way with the Ever-Present One and family. Many of these occasions we can address in our regular weekly worship event, but many are better attended to at a special time, and perhaps a special place.

Worship events prompted by special occasions in our lives provide highlighted opportunities for the embodiment of gospel—for the event of God's loving self-giving—to become particularized for individual persons in the context of specific life-moments and in the context of community. But we do not always articulate clearly what we expect of these services, and we do not always grasp what truly happens.

"Wasn't it a beautiful wedding?" we have all heard guests gush as they leave the church. Perhaps we have said this ourselves. No doubt the wedding has been beautiful, what with flowers, exquisite apparel, and the beaming faces of participants that commonly brighten such an occasion. Why should we not delight in this gift of beauty? Love is a beautiful thing, finding a suitable partner is a precious gift, and being able to gather a community to celebrate with gives great joy. But that the wedding satisfies our aesthetic sense misses the point of celebrating a relationship within a service of worship. Would that the guests exclaim, "What a faithful-to-gospel worship event this has been!" I do not expect to hear such a response. Nevertheless, I am committed to the notion that the specific nature of the event, be it celebration of relationship, funeral, or ordination, is not the primary concern for that event. The ultimate consideration remains the same as that for Sunday worship gatherings: that the event engage all in loving, dialogical relationship with God and neighbor.

Such relational worship depends not only upon God and the particular individual(s) occasioning the worship, but upon the community participating in it. Consequently we need to involve participants in planning and implementing all worship events. It seems unthinkable that we would not involve in creating the worship event those whose very life situation occasions it. In preparation for a celebration of a partnership, for example, pastors commonly engage in conversation with the couple about the character of the wedding ceremony. That we do the same for other events such as an ordination or funeral is simply common sense. But the particular worship event does not *belong* to the pair, the ordinand, the family of the deceased. Rather, it is God's gift to the whole community, a gift endeavoring to embrace all in the divine arms even while it pays particular attention to specific persons and occasions. The whole community, then, serves as an essential source of the development of the whole of whatever the particular service might be. Along with addressing the particular realities of the specific individuals occasioning the service, then, such a worship event needs to crafted with equal care for *all* present, so that it can serve first and foremost as an occasion of loving, dialogical relationship with God and neighbor for *all* who come.

I am not convinced we have done this very well. Traditional marriage services have frequently suggested implicitly or explicitly that marriage is the only truly suitable way of living.[1] They do so at the painful expense of

---

[1] The basis for such is the questionable premise that marriage is part of the "universal order of creation," a notion presumably supported by Mark 10:2–12 or parallels. See, for

those whose lives follow different patterns, e.g., those who are single, whether by choice or default, or those who are committed to gay or lesbian partnerships. Ordination services have often left the impression that the so-called ministry of word and sacrament is somehow "holier" than farming, nursing, or parenting—thereby trivializing people who are not ordained and devaluing other honorable vocations—all of which, Calvin reminds us, are God-given. Funeral services can too easily reflect the assumption that the majority of the congregation is there to support the bereft and are thus able to sing wholeheartedly and joyously hymns of resurrection when, in fact, the whole community may be all but drowning in grief that is given no room for expression. Or, funerals may neglect altogether the fact that the prevalent feeling may not be grief, but confusion, anger, relief, or joy.

We need to ask who else, in addition to the particular individuals whose life experience occasions this event, will be present? What realities inform their lives? How can we help them to experience the loving embrace of God on this occasion? Ongoing conversation with our congregations about our worship life together includes more than our ordinary Sunday worship events, and conversations about particular worship moments needs to include more conversation partners than those occasioning the service. Particular human seasons and experiences, even if encountered randomly by different individuals over long periods of time, are part of our whole life together, and, thus, part of our worship life together.

Birth

We begin our life with God at least at birth; our life of relationship with a whole world full of God's beloved family at least as soon as we leave the womb. It is for many a joyous moment. Some congregations mark it with a rose placed in full view of the congregation and with prayer for the newborn and family. Yet birth can also be a traumatic event. Pregnancy and the processes of birth can radically undermine the mother's body, mind, spirit. The child leaving the warm, cushy, dark womb for the harsh realities of technological society may find such transition scarring. Birth can traumatize the father and siblings as well as others who have to make radical adjustments in their ways of being and doing now that a new infant has arrived. Learning of a birth can create deeply conflicted emotions for those who despair over their own opportunity or ability to bring a child to life or even adopt, for those who are pressured to become

---

example, Philip H. Pfatteicher, *Commentary on the Lutheran Book of Worship* (Minneapolis: Augsburg Fortress, 1990), 456, or the *Service Book for the Use of Ministers Conducting Public Worship* (the United Church of Canada, 1969), 196.

parents when they do not have that vocation, for those whose children may be unhealthy, or dying, or gone.

A rose and a prayer for the newborn and family will not suffice, then. Faithfulness to gospel invites us to find ways to more completely include all the realities of procreation or nonprocreation in our worship life. Our prayers for those affected by such an occasion ask us to stand in solidarity with all of them, and not just for one day only. Gospel encourages us to help one another actively commit to the ongoing nurture and support for the newly born, and for all who are touched—joyfully or painfully—by any particular birth.

The baptism of infants born into our particular branch of God's family can fruitfully serve as the public honoring of the realities expressed at birth. First and foremost of these, as suggested in chapter 2, is that this child, like all children born, comes to life as God's beloved child, a gift to the world, already a member of our community for whom we have the responsibility and privilege of helping live life gracefully. Such a birth/baptismal celebration would affirm the steadfast and life-giving presence of God-with-us through all of our lives, no matter how difficult, no matter how complex, no matter how wonderful. As part of our larger economy of worship life of embodying the reality of God's all-embracing love, such a celebration of birth/baptism would point to and reaffirm our commitment to love-as-ourselves each and every individual whether or not they are part of our particular gathering, because the waters of the womb *are* the waters of God through which all of us come to being and all of us live.

Affirming Faith

So also an occasion of affirming faith needs to honor its larger dimensions. Churches "confirm" youngsters for all sorts of reasons, few, if any of which hold up either to theological or practical scrutiny. Mine certainly didn't. Affirmations of faith, on the other hand, can occur all through an ordinary worship event. That is, if we perceive prayer as Luther did, as an honoring of God in the seeking of God, as a turning of the heart toward God and God's own at the prompting of the Spirit, we can recognize *each moment* of worship as "faith-ing," as participating in loving, dialogical relationship with God and neighbor. Meanwhile, specific opportunities for those who wish for a particular chance to say yes publicly to God and neighbor for the first or sixty-first or two-hundred-sixty-first time can happen at any time. Such events need not be tied to catechesis, age, communion, or anything else. Repentance and faithfulness is a *life-long* struggle in which we are sometimes wheat, sometimes weeds, and catechesis is a never-ending process of faith seeking understanding for the enrichment of our lives in faith.[2] Thus affirmation of faith may occur any time in the life of the individual or the community, it may occur formally or informally, individually within the community or before it, and it may certainly occur more than once!

Partnership

A celebration of partnership may be the next occasion in the life process. The "traditional church wedding" has really not been traditional for terribly long. Marriages were initially understood as civil contracts to which couples committed themselves long before they were understood to have a particular Christian referent or content. As early as Paul we do begin to see treatment of questions of marriage within the Christian context, but these focus on whether marriage or celibacy is preferable, or what makes a Christian marriage different from any other kind. Fifth- and eighth-century worship history hints at possible liturgical celebrations of weddings, yet it seems that only since the Reformation have rites of pairing regularly been celebrated *in* the church.[3] Even then, clergy functioned—as they still do—on behalf of the government perhaps even more than on behalf of the church.

We will want to take special care, then, to be clear about exactly what our intention is in such a worship event. There is no reason, in my view, for a "church wedding" unless participants experience it as a worship event that embodies dialogical relationship and affirms the partnership to be a relationship not just between the mates, but also with regard to God and the whole family of God. Even then, a couple effects the partnership themselves—pastors do *not* marry or otherwise constitute relationships between couples. Dialogical relationship has no room for anyone to be "given away," for no one is a possession. It does require, proclaim, and empower the reality of distinct persons choosing freely to live in particular grace-filled relationship, each partner honoring the other as a unique person in her or his own right.[4] As well, because any relationship between two persons in some way includes the community, can we not ask the community to commit itself to the ongoing care and nurture of the

---

[2] Even Luther intended his catechisms for the ongoing spiritual exercise of all, no matter whether they were coming to the table for the first or sixty-first time.

[3] The history of theological positions about marriage in Christianity is extremely diverse. Worth reading is *Marriage in the Early Church*, David G. Hunter, ed. tr. (Minneapolis: Fortress Press, 1992).

[4] Gospel thus contradicts the notion, presumably based on Matthew 19:4–6, that two persons fuse into a single identity.

couple? Such commitment fits hand in glove with a community's responsibility for all who enter into its life, whether by birth, adoption, affirmation of faith; for all whose relationships in the community change, whether by death, sickness, partnering, or moving. Perhaps such solidarity of support would provide powerful remedy for all whose relationships are dying for lack of sufficient nourishment with gospel.

All worship events require that we ask whether the content and process remain coherent with this theological core, but services occasioned by new relationships, in my experience, are particularly notorious for gospel inconsistency. What do we embody, for example, when one partner's family and friends sit on one side of church and the mate's on other? When clergy slip in the side door with one partner while the other makes a grand procession for which the congregation stands? When floral arrangements or apparel are excessive, or language is utterly disconnected with contemporary reality? What theology do we evidence when at the installation of a pastor or at a covenanting service the front rows are reserved for clergy; when only clergy are ordained, installed, or covenanted with?

Relationships do come in many flavors and colors, but we often neglect to attend carefully to the many possibilities, to celebrate love wherever we find it, to provide all with the same tender loving care we lavish on a few. Lesbian and gay partners have every gospel reason to expect the church to stand and celebrate with them their commitment to one another. Given the ongoing disparity between rich and poor, perhaps we would do well to celebrate and pray for and with new business partners with the same vigor we celebrate ordinations. And we will rightly celebrate other kinds of relationships: friendships, housemates, business partnerships, or new jobs in the so-called secular world.

We need also to carefully attend to the dissolution of relationships, since there is no guarantee that partnerships of any kind—familial, business, ecclesial—are forever. While that may be God's gift to many, and while we may encourage and support persons toward life-long relationships, the only guarantee we can offer is that the promises of baptism remains ours for a lifetime. Even if a relationship should die, God will not fail to love us and be present with us in our struggle and sorrow. We need to work harder and more creatively to find ways to embody God's continuing love and care for those experiencing dissolution of relationships through divorce, death, job loss, retirement, change in ministry, or even by moving away. All such occasions challenge us to put our money where our mouths are and our lives where our prayers are by carefully and concretely lifting up those whose life-relationships and circumstances change both in our worship events and in our day-by-day worship life.

Health

Illness or injury may come at any age and in any shape or form, and worship events occasioned by them are always appropriate. The very word "disease"—dis-ease—implies an intensification of the sufferer's sensitivity and vulnerability. Some of us, when we suffer illness or pain, become insufferable; others turn into heroes; some of us just look like heroes. All of us, I dare say, need acute pastoral sensitivity and theological thoughtfulness, but mostly we need to experience God standing in solidarity with us in our suffering and bringing us to new life. Words help, but many of us need embodied for us that God does not either want or permit us to suffer. Many of us need embodied for us God's arms cradling us, holding us up, and holding us together. Worship events need to make available such care, and they need to provide us room and media for dealing with rage, confusion, denial. No simple task this.

Common perceptions and the valuing of health do not seem to help us much with this. Jürgen Moltmann suggests that health is not any particular condition of the body or mind apart from the ability to live lovingly—an idea which has a merit if only because it allows for the possibility that people with AIDS or brain damage *can* be healed—enabled to live lovingly. Frankly, I want more than this for them. I want those who are suffering to be so loved that their suffering is simply overruled, banished. I do not want them to be told, nor do I want to hear, that suffering will make us stronger, build our character, make us appreciate health more. Is health, then, the absence of suffering? Perhaps. Yet I am reminded of what I have earlier claimed, that life embraces death, and I think that health must also include suffering. I am not happy with this, but the conundrum will not go away. Thankfully, neither will God!

Whatever our theology of health and healing, we can create worship events that focus always on the love of God for us, on the strength, peace, and comfort that God offers us, on the presence of God with us in our struggle no matter what.[5] Such a worship event may well include healing touch—not necessarily with oil, for a cool hand on a fevered forehead or a warm hand gently enfolding a cold one may do more than rivers of olive oil and a thousand anointings. Yet not everyone wants to be touched or can bear being touched—it is only common sense to ask. Moreover, it may be that the family or friends or community as a whole may need as much or more attention and care as the sick or injured member. Watching

---

[5]On one occasion, a worship team included four healing centers, each with a different focus—on creation, on prayer, on play, on anointing—which worshipers could explore during the service.

a loved one endure surgery or be eaten away by cancer may be more difficult than enduring the surgery or the dying itself.

Surgery provides us with a useful paradigm, since it requires a period of postoperative healing. So also with all worship events associated with particular life-moments and experiences, the ministry of healing will not cease when the worship event is over, but can find embodiment in phone calls and meals prepared, notes sent and prayer lifted up day in and day out for all concerned. Such care may need to go on for a very long time. Indeed, can we ever get enough of love's embodiment?

Death

When death comes, we stand ever in need of affirmation that death is part, but only part, of life. Any worship event needs to witness both death and life, and always I think, gospel requires that we give maximum attention to life. Here that remains true, even while the paradoxical relationship of death and life requires special care. We cannot make assumptions about participants' experiences, perceptions, feelings; but we do need to help all honor feelings of grief, relief, confusion, anger, or even celebration, even as we encourage participants to trust in God's unfailing love for us and presence with us.

Eulogies are common in Canada, I've learned, often replacing sermons altogether. I am not sure what this says about sermons, but neither am I certain if eulogies can bear the weight of loving, dialogical relationship with God and neighbor. Is not the focus of a Christian funeral or memorial service God's love for us that in turn empowers us to love? Even though a loved one's death occasions this worship, does not God beckon us to seek solace in God's embrace and offer us the strengthening of our relationship with God so that we might live on? It does not seem to me that such a worship event has any different agenda than proclaiming and embodying God's love for all. This surely can occur in part through articulating the way in which the person's life evidenced God's graciousness. Yet even if the deceased was an unrepentant scoundrel, we can affirm that nothing is too difficult for God to overcome with love, not even the hardened hearts of those who hung Jesus up on the cross to die, not even death itself. I do not think a eulogy alone can do this.

We cannot determine definitively the correct way of addressing a particular death through worship, for as is true of every other worship occasion, in this one also there are many ways of embodying gospel, and cultural heritage, among other realities, makes strong claims that need gracious address. Nor does the worship life occasioned by this event end when the casket is interred or the body cremated—for our life of relationship with God and neighbor continues. Perhaps most especially in what is for many a barren, transitional time, a congregation needs to be most zealous in its worship endeavors so that the bereft will be so deeply and intensely loved back into the life of relationship with God and community that there will be no doubt at all that God is present with them even in the deepest, darkest hour of the night.

Endless Possibilities

A thousand moments in individual, group, and congregational life may call for particularity of expression in worship. These might include times of critical decision-making, safe return from travels, settling into new homes, attending to the effects of violent crime, life-cycle changes, and the like. In recent years some women have begun to find a celebration of menopause and the turn to a new phase of life to be an important occasion for a particular worship event. I wonder, too, if we were more caring in worship about the transition years from child to adolescent and adolescent to young adult, whole families and communities might be strengthened in living gospel and saved much painful trauma.

Many of these moments and occurrences that occasion particular worship events may most suitably fit into our regular weekly worship gathering. While there may be times and occasions where this is not appropriate, we might be wise to consider carefully what is really important enough to cause us to move outside our regular worship life, or, alternately, how we can expand our worship life to authentically and coherently embrace such special worship events apart from Sunday morning.

Perhaps more than any other kind of worship event, occasional services will exercise our ability to do theology. There will always be extenuating circumstances; always judgment calls. In the face of all of them, the question always stays the same: How can we most effectively allow for the affirmation of God's loving presence to all people in all moments of life, joyous, grievous, or both? How can we most faithfully embody gospel for this people in this time and place?

PART IV

The Arts of Worship

CHAPTER 9

Just Language

"Sticks 'n' stones may break my bones but words can never harm me."
Naaa, naaa, naaa–naaa naaaa…It isn't true. If you have been teased, bad-
gered, or harassed by the school bully, a critical parent, or a hostile spouse,
you know full well that words can reduce the strong to tears, induce nonstop stomach cramps, even damage your whole life. Conversely, receiving
words of praise can generate more warmth than a fireplace, turn tears to
laughter, open windows on wonderful new vistas, and create exciting
new futures. Objectively, words may be innocent signs. But words are
never objective. They are always used by subjects, persons; so words have
power, the power to shape our perceptions of reality, our understandings
of reality—power to shape reality itself.

How many men live cramped, damaged lives, how many suffer heart
attacks or strokes because they were all too often told "men aren't supposed to cry"? It seems to me as if they stuff all their emotions inside until
they can't help but burst. How many South Africans were shut out of
universities, businesses, beaches, life, because generations of Christians insisted that black is the opposite of white, light, right, good, God? How
many women and children suffer physical and psychological abuse because they are still told that the man is the head of the household?[1]

Words name our world, words define our relationships to things and
to persons.

---

[1]The reader will find a thorough discussion of this and related issues in Joanne Carlson
Brown and Carole R. Bohn, eds., *Christianity, Patriarchy and Abuse* (New York: Pilgrim
Press, 1989) and Carol J. Adams and Marie M. Fortune, eds., *Violence Against Women and
Children: A Christian Theological Sourcebook* (New York: Continuum, 1995).

As I reach for an exquisite yellow rose, someone cries out, "Look out for the thorns—they are like needles!" My hand jerks back as if of its own accord. Or, I might say to a new student, "That is our university's president—but she is very down to earth and quite approachable. You needn't feel intimidated by her!" I can see in the student's body attention, tension, and release all in the space of a few syllables. Words do not only name our world. Because they name who we are in relationship, words name us and make us who we are.

When we speak of language, "Being itself is at stake."[2] I am who I am perhaps not totally but certainly because my parents said yes to each other, because they named me Pamela, because of words said about me, words said to me. "Have you ever thought about going to seminary?" asked my college professor, Harris Kaasa. "Absolutely not," I replied. Almost before I knew it, I was receiving my M.Div. degree, being called to ministry, being ordained. "You belong in Ph.D. studies," said Bob Worley, the director of my D.Min. program. "Oh, right," I answered, not the least bit convinced; but as a result of these words, my life changed. I reconfigured interests and goals, old relationships dissolved and new ones came into being, I found myself relocating from the Midwest to Georgia to Canada. I no longer am exactly or perhaps even very much who I was before these words were spoken. You are who you are, perhaps not totally but certainly because of words said to you, words said about you.

Letters and words get us into schools, into jobs, into administrative positions, into personal relationships, into life-changing and personality-transforming experiences. Letters and words release us: "This institution is no longer viable and will close at the end of the year." "Congratulations on your sixty-fifth birthday! Enjoy your retirement." "The verdict is: *not* guilty!" We will never be the same because of the words said and written about us. Never. Words have power to shape lives.[3]

Words are potent, but they are not always true. Words can "*fail* to name," David Buttrick says.[4] Furniture stores and car dealerships have mastered this trick—zero down and no payment for two years! Of course,

---

[2] Fred B. Craddock, *As One Without Authority* (Enid, Oklahoma: Phillips University Press, 1974), 36; reflecting on Heidegger's concept of language.

[3] "Words, I learned from experience, can be weapons, and words can be healing. Words can unite in friendship or sever in enmity. Words can unlock who I am or mask me from others. Two words, 'Sieg Heil,' bloodied the face of Europe…Words sentence to death ('You shall be hanged by the neck'), and words restore to life ('Your sins are forgiven you'). Words declare a marriage dead, and words covenant a life together in love. Words charm and repel, amuse and anger, reveal and conceal, chill and warm…" Walter J. Burghardt, S.J., *Preaching, The Art and The Craft* (New York: Paulist Press, 1987), 6.

[4] Buttrick, *Homiletic*, 8, emphasis mine.

what they don't say is that we have to pay for two cars while only getting one, and surrender our mothers as collateral. Words can also *misname*—"words lie," adds Buttrick bluntly.[5] The only good Indian, Russian, Muslim, Tutsi is a dead one; we will *not* cut social services; read my lips...Millions of lives have been ruthlessly brutalized, shattered, and shoved carelessly aside by words. The world suffers hideous pollution by chemical weaponry, nuclear arms, blood, and the slag of a technological society motivated by greed and geared toward destruction. Violated contracts fill our streets with homeless, helpless, desperate people—most of whom would be tickled pink if they could do without recourse to a food bank, let alone find a job that would support them above the poverty level.

Words can also *un-name,* and, thereby, obliterate. "Children should be seen and not heard," I was told as a child. What that really means is that children have nothing to contribute to human discourse, which further implies they are not human and should be invisible as well as unheard and thus nonexistent—at least until they've grown up. If my students reject me when they issue party invitations to others in class, I might cease to exist for them—out of sight, out of mind. More likely I will become an object of discussion rather than a subject engaging in discussion! But if they name me as a dinner guest, we become accountable to each other—they for seeing I get plenty to eat, I for not starting food fights or kicking other guests under the table.

Words have enormous power: over us, under us, making or breaking us, supporting and affirming us, or denying and negating us, perhaps not alone, but certainly words are powerful. It is all the more so for Christians. We are called to embody always and everywhere the good news of God's love for all—to name God's love, to name every person in our global village as God's beloved, to live out love—for the life of the world and to the glory of God. Thus the language we use in worship, on the subway, at the dinner table is never small talk; it is never a minor concern, because we are dealing with gospel which, as we know, is a matter of life or death.

Biblical Words

What language then, shall we use? What words? We have a whole book of words, the Bible. Surely its words are equal to the task! After all, we call scripture God's word, because in it God reveals Godself to us, because in it we see Christ Jesus, the Word of God enfleshed, walking the roads of Palestine changing people's lives with words—words that were deeds. Yet the words of scripture are *human* words, inspired by God, we

---

[5]Buttrick, *Homiletic,* 9.

may believe, but nonetheless the words are human words, phrases, grammar rooted in the being and doing, the experiencing and perceiving of human beings. So Paul's letters are filled with language cast out of his experience as a one-time Jew and persecutor of Christians. His words reflect his knowledge of the law and the pattern of thinking ingrained in him in the pharisaic schools; they reveal what he knows of those to whom he writes, and he uses his reader's language to mediate God's word.[6] So also the chronicler, Jeremiah, the psalmists, the gospel writers, the apocalypticist use languages particular to their unique times and places: All present their claims about God in idioms as different from one another as British English is from Hutterite English, let alone Innuktituk or Thai.

Not only are the tongues of scripture diverse, their words are thousands of years old—written in languages we no longer speak, out of mindsets and worldviews we no longer own. Even reading scripture right off the page attests to multiple interpretive tasks: translating from Hebrew, Greek, or Aramaic into English, Korean, or Spanish; translating from eighth-century B.C. or first-century A.D. to the year 2000, from Palestine or Babylon to New Orleans, Keokuk, or Vancouver. That says nothing of the interpretive process of choosing *which* text or the interpretive nature of tone of voice, inflection, posture…

Moreover, Fred Craddock notes, "some words simply wear out, some change their meanings, others become obsolete, while many fall victim to vulgarization."[7] Who talks about candlepower in a world of kilowatts, lux, lumens, and lasers? What meaning does firmament have in a universe that knows spaceflight beyond our galaxy and into infinity? How about "gird up your loins?" What do we know about sackcloth and ashes, wineskins old or new? Thee, thou, and thy once were the familiar form used to speak to one's beloved or to one's child. But somehow these turned into pronouns of reverence, distance, and awe, used for God alone. The ordinary and intimate became sacred and distant by virtue of words which got separated from their original intent and meaning.

We cannot just use old words, not even sacred old words. We cannot rely on them to convey their original meaning, we cannot assume that words as linguistic constructs hold truth objectively within themselves. Yes, we perceive God is revealed via these words, but in the end, the words themselves do not matter, the Word/Deed in the word, Godself, matters.

---

[6] Acts 17:22, e.g.

[7] Fred B. Craddock, *Preaching* (Nashville: Abingdon Press, 1985), 198.

Divine Words

When Moses asks God for God's name, Moses gets a verb, an expression of God as action. The tetragrammaton is *not* a noun; it is not a *name* for God—it is *not* a word of thingness, it is about God's *be-ing*. God says, "I am who I am—I will be who I will be."[8] God asks, according to scripture, for no images, perhaps because of the human propensity for confusing "Be-ing" with the image, for making a thing of "I am," for focusing on the thing, and forgetting "I will be." The tetragrammaton seemed nonetheless to become the name of God, because it was deemed too holy to speak. Being able to speak another's name gives us power over that one, a gross impertinence, to say the least, as far as addressing God goes. So speaking God's "name" was taboo, and if speaking the tetragrammaton was taboo, then the tetragrammaton must be God's name.

Yet God must be addressed, and the ultimate choice was "Lord." Ironically, the Elijah story suggests "Lord" is what one calls false gods, those who usurp authority and presume to rule over us.[9] Nevertheless, "I am— I will be" soon *became* "Lord." That left precious little room for any other relationship between us and God besides hierarchical dominance/subservience. Further, "lordship" became identified with divinity, and anyone identified as lord was thus imbued with divinity and the right to rule over any who were not lord. History is littered with the tragic results: the gynecide of women, black slavery, the attempted erasure of aboriginal and poor, and the rape of the earth.

The same thing apparently happened with *abba*, Jesus' word of address to God.

Abba, as we know, means "daddy." But *abba* is *not* a word of thingness, nor a description of the dominance/subjection typical of notions of fatherhood in Jewish tradition, nor a matter of defining God's gender. *Abba* is rather an invitation to intimate relationship,[10] "I am—I will be" being-for-us-and-with-us. Perhaps such intimacy made the powerful righteous squirm, for all too soon transcendence, distance, became more important than immanence, presence. *Abba* became, as if by sleight of hand, Father with a capital F.

---

[8] I can still hear George Landes, now retired as Professor of Hebrew at Union Seminary, speak what was a revelation to me over twenty-five years ago.

[9] I am indebted to my student, Michael Rodgers, now a pastor in the Evangelical Lutheran Church in Canada, for this insight.

[10] See Sallie McFague, *Metaphorical Theology* (Philadelphia: Fortress Press, 1982) 170ff and Elizabeth A Johnson, *Consider Jesus: Waves of Renewal in Christology* (New York: Crossroad, 1990), 57, 108.

We do know a lot more about fathers than about "I am—I will be." Father, like Lord, is something we can get a handle on, because both are part of human experience. "Getting a handle on" also allows us to exercise control both by maintaining a safe distance between us and God, and by dismissing what is not lord or father. Not only did "Father" become God's name, then, but for Christians speaking "Father" turned out to be a mandate rather than a taboo.

There may be many things right about calling God father, but by our almost exclusive use of that noun to identify God, we reduced "I am—I will be" to one dimension, made of God a single thing, put God in a box. We created of God an image, (father-image), quite in spite of the commandment—you shall not make for yourself an idol, whether in the form of anything that is in heaven above, or that is on the earth beneath…(Exodus 20.4f; Deuteronomy 5.8f).

God-in-Relationship-with-Us

The tetragrammaton and all of scripture and, most especially, Christ Jesus, insist God is *be-ing*, not a thing to be grasped, but be-ing-in-relationship-with-us. All of us. Indeed, how wonderful the plurality and fullness of scripture's attestations of God-in-relationship with diverse humanity! God enlivens the world,[11] gives birth to us, names us, nurses us at the divine breast, bonds the divine self to us.[12] God covenants with us as colleagues, supports us like a rock, struggles with us against evil, grieves and repents over us.[13] God walks and talks arm in arm with us, a loving Friend; God feeds, clothes, and shelters us,[14] makes and fulfills promises, heals, comforts, and confronts us.[15] God weeps with us in our pain and sorrow. God does theology with us, breaks bread with us, forgives us our narrow-mindedness and our failure to love. God breathes in us, lives in us, greets us in the faces of our neighbors…

Here is God for and with those who have cried out for mommy or daddy in the night, who have felt the earth shake under us, nearly drowned in anger or guilt, walked a lonely street, danced in joyous community, struggled against the onslaught of exploitation or abuse, hungered, fed, taught, sewed, promised, forgave, loved. Here is God for and with all of us, God-being-for-us as God will be—in a multitude of expressions of the

---

[11] Genesis 1.
[12] Numbers 11:12; Isaiah 66:9, etc.
[13] Hosea; Exodus 32:14; Amos 7:3, etc.
[14] Exodus tradition; Genesis 3:21; Nehemiah 9:21; Psalm 61:4, etc.
[15] Isaiah 66:13; miracle stories.

divine Self; expressions that claim God's equal intimacy with each of us no matter our differences and in spite of our sin.

In Christ, Paul says, there is neither Jew nor Greek, slave nor free, male nor female.[16] God lives intimately with all of us. As members of the family of God, the Indwelling One asks not for homogeneity among us, but intimacy, living in one another's shoes, bearing each other's sorrow and joy, not just knowing about each other's reality, but owning it, living it, no matter how different or painful it may be.

Deadly Language

When our language fails to name the full range of God's being-for-us insofar as we know it, when we focus on just one dimension, everything else begins to disappear. Failing to identify God as One-Who-Embraces-Jewishness, Christians blamed the Jews for Jesus' death, persecuted, ghettoized and dehumanized them into the holocaust. Failing to identify God as Being-of-all-Colors, Christians decided that God is somehow not for and with black people, yellow people, red people, that those people are not connected to divinity; that they are ungodly, inhuman. So Christians have enslaved such folk, stolen their land, broken up their families, ignored them and their pleas for the means of survival.

Similarly, always calling God "Father" but never "Mother" casts God in our minds as male, and images femaleness as having nothing to do with divinity. Consequently, women have been seen as "the Devil's Gateway"[17] and "not the image of God."[18] Women have been bought and sold as property, ignored in the church, denied our God-given places as full members of the body of Christ and the priesthood of all believers. To this day women still are trivialized and mocked because we are not male, because we are not close to God because God is "Father." Those who disbelieve this need only note the fierce resistance to naming God "She," to replacing scripture's deadly words about *King*doms, to finding better words than "Lord" to address the one who stands with us and gives away all power over us—who is our *Friend!*[19] For 2,000 years the church has been complicit in death-by-words—and now, perhaps, in its own death.

---

[16] Galatians 3:28.

[17] Tertullian, "On the Apparel of Women," 1,1, in *Ante-Nicene Fathers*, Vol. 4 (Grand Rapids: Eerdmans, 1965).

[18] Augustine, "de Trinitate," 12,7,10; in *Nicene and Post Nicene Fathers*, Vol. 3 (Grand Rapids: Wm. B. Eerdmans Publishing Co., 1956). Rosemary Radford Ruether conveniently cites the misogynist opinions of other theologians in *Women-Church* (San Francisco: Harper and Row, 1986), 138–9.

[19] McFague, *Metaphorical Theology*, 181ff.

Just Language

Word *is* deed, act that shapes, creates, destroys. Language is a matter of being itself—God's and our own. God asks us *not* to attempt to shape God's being. We have much to confess here. We can begin by affirming that God is being-for-us in multiple ways that transcend what any one word or type of metaphor can express. God does call us to help shape a new reality, a new *social* reality in our world. Gospel tells us that social reality will be constructed by doing justice, loving kindness, loving God and our neighbor as ourselves (Micah 6.8; Matthew 22:37–40).

So Jesus walked the land: human, Jew, young, male, yes. What matters, however, is that Jesus lived "I am—I will be" for and with Samaritans, women, children, liars and thieves, rich folk and poor, pharisees, tax collectors, fisherfolk, sellers of purple goods, centurions, homemakers, lepers…Jesus lived justice of a new kind, lived the love of a God whose being surpasses every norm, lived care, attention, affirmation, and empowering of the least of our sisters, brothers, nephews, aunts. Jesus spoke a language that rearranged lives. He embodied words that cracked social conventions and shattered religious traditions. He lived phrases that dared the comfortable righteous to surrender laws that exclude for love that includes even the least of these my siblings, grandparents, street-dwellers. Jesus' ministry attests that we cannot unquestioningly use words, phrases, linguistic structures of the past, because we do not live with God in the past, but in the present. We do not focus on what *was* but what *is* and *will be*.

We know what God seeks from us. We know language is deed and therefore a matter of justice.[20] In the same way that we build elevators for wheelchair travelers because they, too, are called to join Christian community and minister, we need to find languages that honor all people. As justice dismantles apartheid and cries out against tyrants who keep people from self-governance, as justice resists the wrath of the establishment in order to help marginalized folk regain their identity, their dignity, their freedom, their access to life resources, so our commitment to justice calls us to transform our language.

Using just language is like working to rid our streets of drugs that destroy endless lives, like fighting against systems that keep the majority of the citizens of the "two-thirds world" in gross poverty, without enough food, shelter, clothing. Justice refutes the acceptability of patriarchal language and claims women's right to recover herstory, in her words, and to experience full equality in every venue. It affirms that both hetero- and

---

[20] James F. White, "The Words of Worship," *Christian Century*, December 13, 1978, 1202f.

homosexual orientations are gifts of God and strives to enable all persons to live in loving, just relationships. Justice begs us to shape our worship events so that in all their languages we faithfully treat the realities of *all* people, including the marginalized, and affirm the female/native/challenged/impoverished and otherwise battered face of God.[21] If we believe in justice—God's justice—then we believe in just language.

Gospel calls us to love our neighbor as much and in the same way *as we love our selves*, our neighbor who may be the last creature on earth we would every want to claim as our neighbor. Gospel sets us free of language which misnames, unnames, dehumanizes any person or group, and so dehumanizes Christ. Gospel releases us from letters which kill.[22] Gospel empowers us to do justice.

We accomplish justice when our words no longer impoverish, violate, and murder by unnaming or misnaming, by belittling or ignoring, by confusing truth with a particular grammar, by limiting God to a single dimension. God, who is bigger than we let ourselves think, does speak to us through the languages of the past, but in prophetic language—in the languages of *our* time—languages that challenge, confront, name our idolatry, our injustice, our sin. God-Beyond-Our-Imagination invites us to use many descriptions for the divine self so that we know no one is excluded from God and none from our relationships. We can speak and effect justice because we are equal members of the same body, because our identities are rooted in love, because we share the same anguish, hope for and call to help bring about peace on earth, freedom, love, real life for all God's family of friends. Love conquers all, and there is life after the death of all our idols!

But there is no time to waste. In a world where the condition of women, children, and the elderly is worsening everywhere across the globe and where racism and hatred of "the other" increasingly give rise to violence, lives are at stake: human lives, and God's life—because God is God-with-us. All of us. Immanuel is, after all, what Gospel is about.

---

[21] We use the plural word "languages" here to address the fact that language is not merely verbal. Gestures, use of space, liturgical structures all communicate something about the nature of our relationship(s) with God, and all need to be examined and redesigned with regard to the concerns raised in this paper.

[22] Romans 7:6; 2 Corinthians 3:6.

Language That Gives Life

The words we use in worship will never be small talk, never a minor matter, but the language of gospel, of God-being-for-and-with-us, all of us. We need to use words that express God's love for everyone alike, in the face of societal, historical, cultural, religious convention. Our phrases and sentences need to set all free from bondage, oppression, trivialization, de-humanization, and sin. Our linguistic constructs need to give life to all alike: young, old, male, female, WASP, Somali, Croatian, differently-abled and differently-hued, persons with AIDS and Olympic athletes, Hindus and atheists, Wiccans as well as Christians. Such language will name each of us in our particularity as God's, enliven us, empower us to live as God's. We need courageous language that shatters idols and lies, language that gives life. What language shall we choose?

CHAPTER 10

Space and Movement

Take some time to look about you. What do you see? You might get up and wander about the space that surrounds you. Feel the texture of the walls and note their color. How do these affect you? Do they calm you, irritate you, bore you? If there is window glass, you might touch it to see how it feels to you fingertips, palm, or nose. You might take off your shoes and socks and let your bare feet discover anew that upon which you walk. Let your eyes move overhead, let your arms follow. If you cannot reach and touch what is there, let your vision awaken in your tactile memories what that which lies above your head feels like to the touch. How does this space affect you? Do the walls press in, does the gently undulating, leafy greenness outside your window beckon you out? Perhaps the space wraps you in comfort and safety, or demands attention, adjustment, repair. What will you do with this space and what it does with you?

Space matters. We know that the moment we trade a hot, crowded, sweaty city for the cool, blue-green refreshment of cottage country, or the endless expanse of the prairies for the astonishing verticality of the mountains. I was born in prairie country with an open horizon stretching before me and the possibility of walking forever. It doesn't take too long before I begin to feel claustrophobic in the mountains, hemmed in on an island. The tall buildings of Toronto hide sunrises and sunsets, and all is not quite right with my world. Would that I could rearrange this space!

Relational Space

Space matters not only because it provides a personal environment, but because it serves as the locus of our being-in-relationship. In the same way that we can only be together in time, we can only be together in

103

space. Even if our locus of relationship is electronic mail, we speak of the medium as cyber*space*. Should we only communicate through that medium, nevertheless, we still all reside in the same place in space, *space*ship earth. We cannot get around it: space *is* where Christians gather for intentional experiences of encounter with Christ, for events of relationship with God and God's family of friends.

Think about the place where you usually go for Sunday worship. What structures, colors, textures do you see? What do they say about God, God in relationship with us, us in relationship with one another and the world? Of course, not everyone experiences a worship space in the same way; yet we must ask these questions and discover, at least, some answers, because patterns and perceptions of worship space shape our worship, at least as much, if not more so, than our worship shapes our space.[1]

Even though we *can* communicate by telephone or e-mail, it is not the same as being face-to-face, eye-to-eye. Preachers and worship leaders do not tape sermons, prayers, or anthems in their congregations' absence to play back in their presence while the worship leaders relax at home over morning caffeine or bounce around on the tennis court! When we deal with death and life, being at arm's length for hugs and help is essential. So in worship we body forth gospel, embody relationship with people, relationship that reveals God's love for us and God's presence with us.

Because most of us inherit our worship space, we often take it for granted, paying attention to it only when repairs are needed or when the space no longer fits. We rarely ask whether the architecture aids gospel or obstructs it, whether the color scheme or the arrangement of furniture helps worshipers participate fully in gospel relationship as guided by engagement with scripture. Yet "looking is part of loving," says Jim White.[2] We can say the same about hearing and touching, as well. The location of participants in a worship event in a particular space matters. So, we need to take particular care about the space and furnishings of worship events and ask questions before we assume last Sunday's arrangement will suffice for this Sunday.

Does this worship event require the use of space, pulpit, table, lectern, chancel? in this arrangement? Do the people need this element in this place as a focus of God's word/act or as a symbol of "the community's trusteeship" of worship and "continuity with all those who have gone

---

[1] The September 1996 issue of *Ecumenism* addresses "The Many Shapes of Sacred Space" from a variety of faith traditions. Each tradition affirms the importance of the role space plays within their tradition.

[2] James F. White, *Introduction to Christian Worship* (Nashville: Abingdon Press, 1990, rev. ed.), 91.

before?"[3] Do you as a worship leader need it to bolster your confidence or your authority or just as a place from which to work? Do architecture and fittings function as aid or obstacle to people fully experiencing gospel as *relationship*—because they suggest God is *not* in our midst—but above us, hidden from us, separated from us, or because they place walls between leader and congregation? Does the character of the worship event of the day suggest different arrangements, perhaps even a different space altogether that will better enable the people to experience gospel?

Spatial Inheritance

Before the church grew large, before small worship spaces turned into cavernous ones, preachers and presiders used to work from a chair, *ex cathedra*. A chair can be informal, homey. Presiders and preachers can get on the same level, eye-to-eye, with folk in the pew, and our chances of engaging in dialogue are enhanced. We can put a chair anywhere it will fit. Of course, in a large gathering, a chair and the person in it may be lost. Indeed, when the church moved from homes to basilicas and cathedrals, it was no longer possible for the people either to see or to hear a preacher. Perhaps that is one reason for the decline of preaching. It certainly is the reason pulpits got elevated, sometimes being hung high on a wall midway down the cathedral.[4] Somewhere along the way the pulpit got "theologized" as the place from which God's word comes down to us, and faithful Christians are even today described as needing to sit "under" the word.

But few of us worship in cathedrals, and many churches have a public address system to help carry even the weakest voice. Yet in many churches, pulpits and preachers in them still hang over us, and we are compelled to look up at them, especially if we sit in the front pews. Perhaps that explains why the front rows in so many churches are empty at a Sunday gathering. We know God's word stands on its own and in our midst. It needs no help from "authoritative" pulpits.[5] Moreover, the authority of worship leaders comes from God-with-us, not from a piece of furniture.

---

[3] Charles L. Rice, *The Embodied Word: Preaching as Art & Liturgy* (Minneapolis: Fortress Press, 1991), 46.

[4] David Smart describes Christopher Wren's plans for churches providing for about 2,000 people to have pulpits on one side wall of the church, "well into the nave," although others preferred the pulpit "in the midst of the church." Smart also notes the necessity for pulpits to be elevated so they could be heard in the galleries. David Howard Smart, *Primitive Christians: Baroque Architecture and Worship in Restoration London*, Th.D. diss., Trinity College, 1997, 178.

[5] So Luther notes not even angels can improve on the authority of the word or the credibility of it—the word must be accepted on its own account. Sermon for the early Christmas service, *LW* 52, 32.

Perhaps an elevated pulpit or any pulpit, perhaps an elevated chancel or any chancel is not our best option. Consequently, many congregations have relocated the center of action and speech to ground level, even into the midst of the pews. Such a move can go a long way toward strengthening our sense of community, interrelationship, shared responsibility, and celebration.

Consider, as well, the kitchen or dining room tables that served the early churches' meal gatherings, tables around which people sat or even reclined. As the church grew and as the meal became less and less a meal and more and more a sacrifice, tables were placed more distant from the people and looked more like altars. Eventually they were fastened to the east wall of the church, and no one was permitted to approach them except the ordained who presided at them with their backs to the people.

The reformers probably delighted in elevated pulpits but mostly deplored altars, and endeavored to return to authentic table gathering. Even so, our tables often look like altars, or at least not very much like tables, and they are often not very functional tables either. Try sitting at one as if you were going to eat a meal like you do at home or in the church hall. I can almost guarantee it will be a revelatory experience! Interestingly, even though many congregations no longer use their inherited pulpits, they may still use the same table, even though it serves no better than the pulpit in speaking and acting gospel relationship.

Living with the Inheritance

Worship events, events of liturgy/preaching, we remember, are occasions of embodying gospel. We engage in a whole-person enterprise—a fact easily missed when all our congregations sit neatly in rows, one behind the other, seeing only the backs of heads, or of the preacher, mostly mouth. Experiencing such Sunday after Sunday makes it easy to think that gospel really belongs only to the head. Perhaps the more preachers get out of pulpits altogether and get fully visible to the congregation, the more often worship leaders get on the same level with the folk and enable all to gather around the table, the more people will recognize that God is present *among* us, that proclaiming gospel is something for all of us to do *together* in the sanctuary and in the ordinary choreography of daily life.

Preachers can preach from the table (rumor has it Calvin did this), from the font, or in a center aisle. They might preach moving from place to place. After all, some of us do our best thinking on the move, and such traveling preaching also underscores the dynamism of gospel. We might relocate the table to the sanctuary floor, turn it lengthwise to locate it in the aisle, replace it with a round one, or invite the whole congregation into another room so we may more truly feast together. We could even unbolt the pews from the floor as my roommate and I did over twenty-five years ago at Union Seminary in New York. We might arrange pews in conversation groupings (like the old box pews), put them in concentric circles or semicircles, or replace them altogether with chairs in order to help enhance gospel relationship.

What use of space, furniture, movement will most fully help the embodiment of gospel in this worship event? These questions, too, are part of the ongoing conversation congregations need to sustain about our whole worship life. That means there really is hope for pews that are bolted down and the table built into the back wall or fenced. A congregation committed to gospel—a congregation that understands worship events to be matters of death or life—will do what must be done to opt for life.

Dance? In Worship?

Space matters to us in worship because it is the locus of exchange of energy, the place where life-movement happens. Yet, at least as far as people in the pew are concerned, most of the movement in worship events is done by someone else. Curiously, sitting in pews while others do things is a relatively recent invention and one that would have been quite out of character in the worship life of our ancestors.

Scripture reveals that God was actively present in Hebrew life, and worship meant *active* involvement of the whole person, the whole community. Painting pictures in sermons, burning incense, and lifting up the hands in prayer were not enough. Many texts in the Older Testament explicitly refer to dance; others do so by virtue of historical context or the literary character of the text.[6] Worshipers engaged the whole body and the entire community in movement that prayed, praised, proclaimed—embodied—worship. Indeed, every segment of human existence seems to have had expression in dancing worship. We see Miriam and the women of Israel dancing thanksgiving for deliverance from Pharaoh's chariots and David and the people dancing the ark to Jerusalem in praise of God (Exodus 15:20; 2 Samuel 6:5, 16). Psalms 30, 149, and 150 refer to dancing, and many more psalms were probably written to be danced.[7] Oracles might have been danced[8] and certainly dancing was part of worship at court. Covenant ceremonies—celebrating the dynamic relationship between God and the entire people, as well as the wholeness and the

---

[6] Hal Taussig, *New Categories for Dancing the Old Testament* (Austin: The Sharing Company, 1981), 3.

[7] Ibid., 12.

[8] Ibid., 14, 18.

all-encompassing nature of being the people of God may well have been danced.[9] Tales told around campfires may have been danced, and when such stories came into worship events, the dance probably came, too. What better way to bring alive the experience of a Joseph being sold into slavery, a Leah compelled to play out a charade, a Shadrach in a fiery furnace?

Other momentous occasions in the life of the Hebrew people included the movement of Wisdom among them. Scripture tells us Wisdom—Sophia—took part in creating the world, giving shape to it, and sharing in primary relationship between people, creator, and universe. Wisdom also animates and shapes all the biblical arts, and especially dance, for Sophia is always on the move as the essence of "life which gives shape to energy."[10] Luke, John, and Paul all see Jesus as Wisdom, Sophia—never still, always on the move, giving life.[11] Many other Newer Testament texts, by form or context, seem related with dance and may have been danced, including hymns and parables. Certainly early Christians worshiped with their whole being. Incarnation leads Paul to say the body is the temple of the Spirit, and that we are to glorify God with our bodies. Perhaps most important, scripture and the gospel it manifests consistently deal not with concepts, but with life bodied forth, with relationship expressed in the fullest way yea, verily, even in dance. How could we fail to understand, then, that life which is bodied forth, life which glorifies God in our bodies, is a life which dances?

Clement of Alexandria, Gregory of Nanzianzus, Ambrose, Chrysostom and Augustine all affirm dancing in worship. They see it as a way of expressing joy that is both inherent and fitting in those living in authentic relationship with God and neighbor, and thus honoring God. We frequently find the word *choros* or *choroi* in early church writings. It means a dance done by worshipers to the chanting of hymns or refrains,[12] while *stanza* has to do with standing, i.e., not moving through this part. How difficult it is to process down an aisle while trying to sing a hymn we don't really know—and note the fact that we stand to sing still.

Through the medieval era, dance abounded in the church. Even in moments of deepest despair, Christians could not forget Jesus had walked,

---

[9] Ibid., 21–22.

[10] Hal Taussig, *The Lady of the Dance* (Austin: The Sharing Company, 1981), 9.

[11] Taussig, *The Lady of the Dance,* 17–18. See Luke 2:40; 1 Corinthians 1, 2:7; and John. In my view, the best address of Jesus as Sophia is found in Elizabeth A. Johnson, *She Who Is: The Mystery of God in Feminist Theological Discourse* (New York: Crossroad, 1992).

[12] Margaret Taylor, "A History of Symbolic Movement in Worship," in Doug Adams and Diane Apostolos-Cappadona, eds. *Dance as Religious Studies* (New York: Crossroad, 1990), 16–19.

talked, eaten, and yes, danced with them, loved them enough to die for them, and provided them with indestructible hope in the promise of God's continuing presence with us. Their jubilation was sufficient to enable them to dance even in the face of the black plague.[13] Do you remember as a child singing and dancing to *Ring around the Rosie, pockets full of posies, ashes, ashes, we all fall down?*

Growing Immobility

The very nature of congregational dance is intimate contact with Christ who dwells within and among us. Its very character is that of the equal and familial nature of relationships with God and each other—rather like a square or line dance! Not surprisingly, as the ecclesial hierarchy took increasing control of worship as part of the design to keep the mundane from profaning the sacred, the councils attempted to restrain dance in worship. Dance became less spontaneous, and some forms were excluded. Along with practically everything else in a worship event, the clergy finally reserved dance in worship for themselves.[14] We can still see in the bowing, genuflecting, signing, and elevation characteristic of Roman Catholic worship the dance of a choreographed liturgy.

Meanwhile, the enlightenment's emphasis on reason and intellect pushed the body into disrepute, hiding it away in Victorian dress and mores.[15] By the nineteenth century, congregational and sacred dance had all but disappeared from worship events. In some places in Europe, however, the carol was still a dance with singing. The Shakers used dance in worship, stepping together across the floor, holding out their hands to shake off sin as we might shake off water in the absence of a towel and then turning the palms face up while continuing the shaking movement to receive the gifts of God.[16] Dance appears with frequency in numerous congregations in North America today. Nevertheless, immovable pews in innumerable churches attest that for many, movement and worship really have nothing to do with each other.

Embodied persons live out our relationship with God and God's people. We embody gospel, or we embody something else. If we always sit virtually immobile in the pew while speaking words of jubilation or talking of love, what do we truly express? The stranger will always make the same decision about which speaks louder, our actions or our words.

---

[13] Doug Adams, *Congregational Dancing in Christian Worship* (Austin: The Sharing Company, 1971), 116.

[14] Doug Adams, *Congregational Dancing*, 45–49.

[15] How intriguing I find the continuing prevalence of vestments that all but obscure the body!

[16] Taylor, *Dance as Religious Studies*, 30.

Bringing the Body Back to Life

Some of us are called to interpret scripture and express relationship through individual or small group movement done amid a congregation and on a congregation's behalf. Such dance intends to call the community into an experience of God-with-us[17] much in the same way an instrumental prelude or a choral anthem does. Yet each of us is invited to worship God with our whole being, and if we can breathe we can, in some way, dance. Almost everybody can tap a toe or nod a head, almost everybody can clap, sway right and left in concert with our neighbors, or join hands and move in a circle of the all encompassing love of God. Most of us can travel two or three abreast and so declare that together we are about the business of bodying forth God's love in the world. Different cultures may provide other kinds of movement that can faithfully be brought into worship events to enhance our relational life.[18] In any case, what matters is not who is graceful, rhythmic, imaginative, or beautiful to watch. What matters is that movement—like preaching, prayer, music—is a gift that enables us to embody all aspects of our life in relationship with God.

Gospel sets us free to express the affection of our hearts in rich, lively movement, movement that will enact a love that gathers others into our life, not just in our heads or with our voices, but with all that we are, embodied members of the family of God's friends. But it is precisely gospel that moves us, not law. We want movement that graciously embraces God's people, and invites us to dance in faithfulness to gospel and each other as members of the one body. Arthritis or the pain of grief can make movement not an enactment of love and praise but an act of torture. Anything more than the clasp of hands may do violence rather than surround in love the victim of sexual abuse. Moreover, many of us are a long way from freedom from culturally shaped limits on body discourse, from the idea that our bodies are the tools of the devil and thus must always be restrained, controlled, hidden, and certainly not used as a medium of worship.

We need to help one another recognize the appropriateness and the necessity of embodying worship. We do that not by imposing unusual movement on a gathered community, but by inviting each other into worship preparation and development processes that truly honor

---

[17] Judith Rock and Norman Mealy, *Performer as Priest & Prophet* (San Francisco: Harper & Row, 1988), 42. See also Judith Rock, *Theology in the Shape of Dance: Using Dance and Worship in Theological Process* (Austin: The Sharing Company, 1978), 7.

[18] See, for example, Elochukwu E. Uzukwu, *Worship as Body Language: Introduction to Christian Worship: An African Orientation* (Collegeville: The Liturgical Press, 1997).

incarnation and occur not just in our heads, but in and through our bodies. In study group or sermon preparation group or worship committee we can help one another explore scripture readings through movement, inviting each other to move freely to text or music or prayer, letting them know that our many everyday movements can profoundly speak gospel, that it can be appropriate to sway or tap toes or clap hands, to gesture, walk, spin, or jump in discovering and expressing a text. Preachers need to ensure that sermons are rooted in embodiment, the preacher's own and the congregation's. We can see to it that our movement and use of space in the whole of the worship event arise out of that embodiment, that our embodiment is thus coherent with gospel, that our movements articulate as clearly as our words, whether the words of sermon, peace, bath, or hymn. We will ensure that our gestures are loving, that they invite, enliven, empower each other to the richest possible life of living out the love of God.

Our movements *will* speak for us; the question is only what and how well they do so. Meanwhile, gospel invites us into a rich and life-giving choreography. How can we resist?

CHAPTER 11

Music

The church in which I grew up sang a great deal. I sang hymns and service music in the pew, hymns and anthems in choir, and hymns at home. I discovered quickly that while speech is a whole body endeavor (usually a stiff body when reciting my Christmas "piece"), when you sing the body gives so much more and so much more freely. Toes tap, diaphragm pushes, muscles of mouth and throat work harder; you nod, sway, bounce, or even dance. Perhaps, if you sing only minimally, you have never noticed. But if you sing from the depth of your soul, you cannot miss the impact of this whole-person engagement. Singing Handel's *Messiah,* Beethoven's Ninth, or even a collection of favorite hymns can leave us both exhilarated and exhausted, having worked as hard, perhaps, as a gymnast or marathoner.

Music manifests the relationship in which God embraces God's creation and serves as a fundamental medium of conversation with God and neighbor. It is a basic mode of creaturely expression: crickets chirp, loons cry, whales sing, and we whistle in the dark. As a particularly human expression, music offers us not only notes and rhythms, but also words. With music we do not simply say something straight out. Instead we color our everyday speech with rainbows and give it wings; we empower our passions with pitch and meter. Music is a particularly human thing, too, because instruments can become extensions of our being. We can push wind through tubes, press organ keys to sound pipes, put drumsticks to drum, or stroke the strings of violin or harp. What would our lives or world be without music?[1]

---

[1] Obviously I ask this question as a hearing person. As a hearing person, I also find the art of signing for the culturally deaf profoundly musical.

Belonging

Music belongs to all of us. Even the deaf can feel a beat and learn to dance. Many years ago I participated in a dance class that was privileged to have a completely hearing-impaired student in the group. The soles of his feet served as ears, for through them, he told us, he could "hear" the beat. Even hearing persons sometimes can feel apart from our ears the impact of a drum, the roar of a jet, or a piercing whistle. Yet music is also *intrinsic,* as basic as the beating of our hearts, or the keening of our souls when we mourn. We may indeed hear this internal music, but we also feel it. Part of the reason for this may be that music is not only a matter of sound, but also of silence. Composers pepper musical scores with rests— places where no sound happens—not only because musicians must breathe sooner or later, but because sound and silence together shape a melody, a chord, a hymn, a symphony of psalms. We hear and can feel not only the changes produced by sound waves, but also by the stopping of sound waves. Sound and silence create physical sensations not only through the ears, but through the wholeness of our being and thus shape us musically.

Music belongs to worship, because sound and silence are God's gift to us, because music has to do with what it means to be human, with being in relationship with God and God's creation. Are we happy? asks the author of the epistle to James. Let us sing a hymn of praise. Are we in pain or sorrow? Who of us has not, then, sung hymns of lament or hymns that comfort us? Are we thankful? We might sing "Come ye thankful people come, raise the song of harvest home," or perhaps "Amazing grace…" If we are confused, we may sing through our whole repertoire! Every human experience, every mood, every kind of relationality finds its expression in music, in plain chant or eight-part harmony, via electronic keyboard, drum, or full orchestra and choir.

Music also functions to enhance solidarity. When we sing together, we not only say words together, we make the effort to match notes and rhythms, to find ourselves caught up in the ebb and flow of multiply produced sound waves. We listen to one another, attend to what the other is doing, all the more so if we play or sing harmonies! We may not experience this if we sing indifferently, but if our music *is* prayer, an affection of the heart, we can raise a roof and change the world by the power of making music *together.*

There will be times when our heart is so burdened we cannot sing, when tears choke us, when our only song is the silent echoing of grief within or the slow sizzle of the fires of held-down anger. We stand mute while the community sings, but even so we are part of the song, if only by virtue of remaining within the range of auditory movement. More likely we will participate through the blood thumping through our veins in time or via the rhythmic inhale/exhale that funds both those who sing and those who keep silence.

Echoes from the Past

No wonder the church has almost always worshiped with music. Scripture, particularly the Older Testament, is full of references to instrumental and vocal music in worship events. The Newer Testament does not lack musical referent, either.[2] Paul and Silas sang hymns in prison; Mary, Simeon, and the Corinthians sang; the community that generated the Book of Revelation abounded in sung amens and alleluias. The medieval Cathedral mass was a feast of music, but the church seemed to have forgotten that not only the freedom to hear, but also to do, music in worship belongs to all of us. The reformers despaired of masses with extravagant concert performances that gave the people no opportunity to sing; they despaired of professional choirs so perfect that they made ordinary folk ashamed to sing and made the choir rather than the people's relationship with God the focus of the event. In order to provide a remedy, Luther and Charles Wesley wrote congregational hymns, Calvin claimed the psalms for the people to sing, Biblical canticles reappeared, prayers got set to music. Generations of hymnals have followed, shaped by Christian faith and shaping it, perhaps doing as much to immerse us in theology as any other single component of a worship event, including the much-vaunted preaching.

Music as Theology

Yet just because a hymn is in print or a canticle is set does not necessarily mean we should sing it. Just because an old beloved hymn surrounds us with the warmth of the family gathered about the piano when we were children does not necessarily mean that hymn is suitable for our worship life today. Hymns serve us, like lectionary texts, as resources, but it is up to us to determine if and when we might appropriately use a hymn in community. A key factor in making that decision is theology. More than an expression of emotion, more than an aid to our being in community, music as a gift from God functions in relation to gospel. A hymn or even an instrumental work has the capacity to become an event of relationship, of God offering loving embrace to us and all humankind

---

[2] We may find fewer references than we expect, however, because neither Hebrew nor Greek contains a distinct word for music. Speech and singing were simply not compartmentalized as they are today. J. Gelineau, S.J., "Music and Singing in the Liturgy," in *The Study of Liturgy*, rev. ed., Cheslyn Jones, Geoffrey Wainwright, Edward Yarnold, S.J., Paul Bradshaw, eds. (London: SPCK, 1992), 497–98.

and humankind responding with a resounding AMEN! Music can also do the reverse, obstructing or even refuting gospel, fostering death rather than life.

Not just any music will do, then, but that which proclaims God for us, that names our reality in light of God's love, that enables us to live manifesting love in the world. Does this text empower life-giving relationship? Does it participate in faithful dialogue with the gospel core of the day; does it relate appropriately with scripture, sermon, and the order of the day? What are worshipers to think if the words of the hymn qualify or contradict the content of the sermon? What are we to believe if the content of the rest of the service blooms with the joy of Easter but the hymn comes "out of the blue" with lament or judgment?

Music as Technical Art

We must look at the melody and harmony as well. A frivolous tune can go a long way toward making gospel look like a nursery rhyme; a well-constructed one can enliven gospel quite beyond, and sometimes even in spite of or entirely without words. So also a tune that is difficult to sing can obstruct relationship. One that enables us to pour our all into it can create an extraordinary solidarity in love. Moreover, an organist, pianist, drummer, or brass player who overwhelms us with power, speed, volume, or pizzaz can abolish inclusiveness. A musician who encourages and supports us can enable us to know that the commonwealth of God is at hand. Similarly, because music is given to all of us, if there is a choir, it will work mostly to enable the congregation's song. Musicians aid our music and our worship by providing us with instrumental support, by modeling the excellence we would have in all our endeavors of the heart, by teaching us new music, and by singing and playing for us when we cannot sing ourselves, what we cannot sing ourselves.

Although music is a primordial means of human being, a constitutive part of our relationships, although music can proclaim and enable the event of graced relationship, not everything in the worship event needs to be suffused with the sounds of music. For instance, perhaps we would be more faithful to our commitments if the offering was gathered in silence rather than under cover of sound; if we were given a period of intensive silence after the blessing to consider our next steps rather than being immediately surrounded by a postlude. Nor is worship without any constructed music—preludes, anthems, chants, hymns—necessarily antithetical to gospel. Our Loving Liberator surely offers us freedom *not* to sing or play if doing so is inauthentic or impossible for us at a given time or if our endowment of gifts does not include the making of music. Indeed, Quaker communities worship weekly without hymnody or other such music, and they surely worship as faithfully as any of the rest of us. But for most of us most of the time, the sounds and acts of music will remain part and parcel of our worship events, because relationship with God and others so widely lives itself through music.

Easing the Way

Worship leaders need to be intentional about developing their own gifts of music to the best possible degree. They need to work at enabling a congregation to make good decisions about which music is used and how it is used. Every worship planning group will want to ask if this music coheres with gospel and connects appropriately with its partners in the worship event. They will want to choose hymns that use language accessible by the congregation, with metaphors and images that can engage people living in this particular time, place, and circumstance in the depth of gospel. This means examining carefully *every* verse before assigning a particular hymn a place in a worship event!

Along with concern about theological content, we cannot minimize the need for a hymn to be truly singable by a particular congregation. If its melody is strange to us, or its range exceeds our grasp, or the fit of words to notes defeats us, the hymn will probably not empower conversation with God, build relationships, or enable a community to manifest God's love in the world. Sometimes the hymn can simply to be left to others to sing, but helping congregations learn new music may be one of the most worshipful things we do.

As with all elements of worship, the particular character of a congregation determines the manner in which we can introduce new music. Context makes a world of difference, and so there can be no single "right" way of helping a community to explore and faithfully critique new (or old) musical resources. A community's ongoing conversation about worship naturally includes the use of music. As well, new hymns, can be introduced as an anthem and played as prelude, offertory, or postlude for several weeks prior to inviting a congregation to sing them. Having been introduced to the hymn by ear in this way, we will find it easier to sing because it already retains an air of familiarity. Alternately, a song leader can line out a new piece—singing a phrase or line while the congregation listens, then singing the same line over again with the congregation, working through the whole in this way.

There are probably as many ways to learn new music as there are kinds of music to learn. Indeed, becoming comfortable and valuing multiple styles of music in worship can expand our worship life significantly.

Music need not be tried and true to enable gospel relationship, nor must it have the capacity to last forever to be valuable in our worship life. Contemporary music and ancient music, harp, organ, electric guitar, or synthesizer can all give life to our worship and to our world if they are brought thoughtfully into our experience. But if, by virtue of the capacity of the music or instrument, of the player or singer, or of the ears of those who will hear, the music cannot function this way, gospel frees us and beckons to find another piece, another possibility.

Even as I write, my parakeet is burbling happily away, singing his little songs of praise. He also talks, often in full sentences. On other occasions, song and speech tumble forth with the astonishing exuberance and honesty of a tiny heart filled to the brim with God's mystery. Then this little bird's words don't necessarily make sense, but together with his song, he wings to us bigger folk an essential reminder. Perfection in choice or execution of music does not constitute the final act when it comes to relationship with God and God's family of friends. What matters, as with prayer, is the turning of the heart to God and neighbor, and singing, speaking, or simply breathing the depths of one's being, prompted by the Spirit who sings within us, and dressed in the best gift we have to offer. "If you have only one note," Don Saliers has said, "sing it with conviction!"[3]

---

[3] For several years while I was a doctoral student at Emory, I heard Don introduce new students to Sunday morning worship in Cannon Chapel with these or similar words. The music of worship on those mornings was always vigorous and rich, if not always perfect!

CHAPTER 12

The Visual, the Tactile, the Symbolic

Movement and music are not the only arts fundamental to human life and belonging to worship. Everywhere we turn we find ourselves surrounded by the visual and tactile arts: painting, sculpture, carving, weaving. Aesthetic objects, says Webster's Ninth, have to do with beauty. I think of an exquisite crystal bowl I once saw at Tiffany's, of Monet paintings, the sculpture of the crucified woman that stands outside what was once my office window. I think of hand-thrown and uniquely glazed pottery, and the exquisite tapestries and weavings made by the indigenous folk of South America. In our churches we may see carvings on lectern and pulpit, finely stitched paraments, Rose windows, the earthy beauty of lovingly crafted wooden offering plates, or the exquisite richness of deeply burnished metal chalices. Everywhere around us we can see expressions of beauty, art.

And then, as if to keep us from being carried away by ecstasy, a Picasso or Andy Warhol pops into view or more likely a billboard, advertisement, reminding us that art may have little if anything to do with beauty—or at least beauty as we commonly think of it. Yet some of these works may be understood as art not because of any relationship to beauty—whatever that really is—but because they express something essentially human, something words cannot say: "Art is a disclosure of being," says David Power.[1] So we may be compelled by a gallery full of photographs of natural disasters

---

[1] David N. Power, *Unsearchable Riches: The Symbolic Nature of Liturgy* (New York: Pueblo, 1984), 203.

or impoverished women to learn something new about our own identity and role.

Religious Ambiguity

Presumably, "religious" or faithful art also expresses something that has to do with our relationships with each other and with God. Art may fit the category of "religious" because it visibly or tactilely expresses something about that which is "holy"; or because it is motivated by the relationship of love and dialogue that we share with God and neighbor, even though the piece of art may itself not have an apparent religious motif. One might, e.g., paint a grapevine because one is moved by the relationship of trunk to branches, seeing there a model of our relationship with God and world. Yet a viewer, especially one unfamiliar with the Johannine text that speaks of Jesus as the vine and the followers as branches, would not necessarily know the grapevine had a religious meaning unless the motivation behind the painting were somehow disclosed. So also, one might sculpt a scene of table fellowship with Christ. Even though the subject is a "religious" one, if the artist created it out of anger or in mockery, we may have cause to question if it is truly "religious" art. Still, if we consider all creative ability to be a gift of God, then all art, no matter how well or how poorly done, according to whatever criterion, if it honors the ability and is done as an affection of the heart toward God and/or other, can surely be deemed "religious."[2] Yet again, no matter how exquisite a piece or religious the theme, if a work is conceived maliciously then are we not constrained to reckon it sin?

Can we look at a *Pieta* or a Calder mobile apart from the intention of the artist? Can we assume the artist's intent is visually accessible in the work and thus determinable? And what of the truism, "beauty is in the eye of the beholder"? What may be for me a profound expression of gospel in stained glass may be for you nothing short of idolatry. The possibility, if not the fact of idolatry, is why some of the reformers became iconoclasts, removing every shred of art from churches, allowing only the barest, most functional vestments and utensils to remain. They perceived that for many, rather than enabling the conversation between congregation, God, and world, art had become at best a distraction from relationship, and at worst, the work of art had become the place on which the people

---

[2] Geoffrey Wainwright, following Tillich in *Theology and Culture*, says "a religious dimension remains present in all artistic creativity." Geoffrey Wainwright, *Doxology: The Praise of God in Worship, Doctrine, and Life. A Systematic Theology* (New York: Oxford University Press, 1980), 365.

hung their hearts.[3] The community had come to confuse the object with God—the art itself had become the focus of their adoration and thus idolatrous.

We do need art that expresses and helps us in our connection with God and God's people, art that functions to aid us in recognizing the extraordinary love of God for us, art that proclaims the realm of God and that empowers our relationality. If it does not do this, or when it no longer meets this or similar criteria, no matter the external beauty of the piece, no matter the intention of and affections of the artist, we need to inquire vigorously if the art belongs any longer in our worship events.[4]

Iconography

The Eastern church values a unique form of art: iconography. Although many Western Christians are not familiar or comfortable with this kind of art, it can help us to a renewed appreciation of all kinds of art as media of loving, dialogical relationship with God and neighbor. An icon is a painted image that represents in a caricatured way Christ, Mary, a martyr, or other individual whose life was exemplary or foundational for the community of faith. An icon can inspire viewers to similarly faithful lives and offer a visible witness of doctrine and holiness,[5] particularly for those who cannot read.[6] These paintings can affirm and remind us of the incarnation and serve as a means of venerating that which the icon represents, which is, in all cases, ultimately God.[7] An icon may also clarify the meaning of the divine liturgy. Icons, then, are intended to enable

---

[3] Luther says in his discussion of the First Commandment, "That to which your heart clings and entrusts itself is, I say, really your God." "The Large Catechism," 365. Again, in his "Commentary on the 'Sermon on the Mount'" *Luther's Works*, Vol. 21 (St. Louis: Concordia, 1954) he references the source text of Matthew 6:21("For where your treasure is, there your heart will be also.") and attributes to Augustine, "Whatever I love, that is my god." 190.

[4] So Vatican II accepts those works which "aim exclusively at turning men's [*sic*] thoughts to God persuasively and devoutly," *Documents of Vatican II*, Abbott, 174. *Environment and Art* draws two criteria: Quality—love and care, honesty, integrity, wholeness in making; appropriateness: "capable of bearing the weight of...awe" and of serving, 14–15. See also Joanna Weber, "The Sacred in Art: Introducing Father Marie-Alain Couturier's Aesthetic," *Worship* 69/3 (May 1995): 243–262.

[5] Constantine Kalokyris, "The Content of Eastern Iconography," *Concilium* 132, David N. Power and Luis Maldonado, eds. (Edinburgh: T & T Clark; New York: Seabury Press, 1980), 9–10.

[6] St. John Damascene, "Concerning the Holy Icons," in Constantine Cavarnos, *The Icon: Its Spiritual Basis and Purpose* (Haverhill, Massachusetts: Institute for Byzantine and Modern Greek Studies, 1973).

[7] So claims Cavarnos in his Introduction to *The Icon*. Cf. the 7th Ecumenical Synod, "Concerning the Holy Icons," this reverence is not the "true worship (latreia) of faith, which pertains to the divine nature alone." N.p.

people to participate more fully in the worship event.They certainly represent more than paintings valued in their own right as works of art, for icons, like signs, point beyond themselves to another referent.[8] As well, icons enable worshipers to participate in the reality to which the icons point.An icon is thus a symbol, that which both points beyond itself and participates in the reality to which it points.

Symbol

Symbols embody "real" "as its very expression and mode of manifestation," says Alexander Schmemann, but symbols do not necessarily (if ever) contain the whole of that reality, nor do they lose their own intrinsic reality.[9] That is, while our carved grapevine bespeaks Jesus as the vine from which the branches grow, it remains at the same time a carving of a grapevine. So also, baptismal water is ordinary H_2O.Yet that same water, in baptism, can connect us with the waters of the womb, the water of washing, the water of quenching thirst, and of sustaining life. It can connect us as well with the devastation of flood or tornado, hurricane or, yes, drought.

Symbols, like metaphor, present both an "is" and an "is not."We speak of the bread on the communion table as the body of Christ.Yet we know that Christ is not contained in the bread.Augustine, we recall, in addressing his newly baptized members, orients them toward the table and says, "there *you* are on the table..."[10] The newly baptized are not literally on the table. But with such language, Augustine names the bread as that which empowers our becoming bread for the world, and makes of the bread a vision of how we are to live. Ordinary bread becomes "more" than ordinary bread; a "more" that is bound up in belief, in tradition, in the phenomena of our gatherings, in the impact of eating this bread in the company of those present, in a world where many go hungry and some starve to death.

In the intersections of relationship that we call faith, an idea, an act, a thing, a person *becomes* symbol and takes on a quality that enables something beyond what the bare element or its essence speaks. Symbol is more than a means of understanding reality; it is a means of participating in it at depths beyond the surface level of experience.[11] We may well wonder if symbol is a medium of cognition at all or rather divine mystery which

---

[8] Augustine,"On Christian Doctrine." Book II, chap. 1 ff.
[9] Schmemann, *For the Life of the World,* 139, 141.
[10] Sermon 229, emphasis mine.
[11] Schmemann, 139.

speaks not to the logical, analytical corner of the brain, but to embodied wholeness, to the affections of the heart, to the deep longing of the soul.

With symbol, we get in over our heads, to the very heart of the matter. Louis Maldonado tells us art endeavors "to make known the secret nature of things."[12] Alexander Schmemann suggests that symbol communicates "the 'other' *as* precisely the 'other,' the visibility of the invisible *as* invisible, the knowledge of the unknowable *as* unknowable, the presence of the future *as* future."[13] Is this knowledge? Or is it encounter with mystery? Is this our cognition resulting from our entering into epiphany as a manifestation of the divine, or is it epiphany surrounding us with experience of itself and which we cannot finally put into words, and so symbols come into being?

Failure of Symbol

We deal here with depths of meaning and experience, with the interrelating of divine and human ecosystems in such profound ways that we finally are reduced to incoherent babble when we try to put it all into words with one-to-one correlation; rightly, as long as symbols retain the tension/polarity of is (immanence) and is not (transcendence). When the reality becomes collapsed in the symbol, when the icon of Christ *becomes* for us the essential Jesus of Nazareth, when the bread *becomes* Christ so that if only for a moment we hold Christ captive there, then we are submerged in idolatry.[14]

Authentic, faithful apprehension of symbol requires particular recognition of the *is* **not** as much as the *is*. But there are failures of symbol that we create apart from idolatry.[15] A symbol may lose its power by accumulating too many meanings or experiences. So, when we include with baptism's water bath creedal affirmations, questions to sponsors, invocations over the water, anointing with oil, lighting and blowing out of candles, giving of salt and a white robe, we may do more to obscure the essence of baptism than to enhance it. Perhaps that is why Christmas and Easter have become such odd events—because we have incorporated into them so many cultural expressions that muddy the waters of birth and new life.

---

[12] Luis Maldonado, "Art in the Liturgy," *Symbol and Art in Worship*, Concilium 132 (Edinburgh: T & T Clark, New York: Seabury Press), 6.

[13] Schmemann, 141.

[14] Power, *Unsearchable Riches,* 70, 75. Cyrille Vogel, "Symbols in Christian Worship: Food and Drink," *Concilium* 132, 67: " The tension and polarity between the significant and the referent must be kept constant. Should the one be identified with the other in any way the result would be a 'reification' or recourse to an act of magic."

[15] Nathan Mitchell, "The Dissolution of the Rite of Christian Initiation," *Made, Not Born: New Perspectives on Christian Initiation and the Catechumenate* (Notre Dame, Indiana: University of Notre Dame Press, 1976).

A symbol may lose its intelligibility because it no longer functions *heuristically*. That is, it can no longer trigger a chain reaction in us that leads us into deeper and deeper recognition of implications: e.g., water—thirst-quenching—death preventing—life-sustaining—life-giving—our responsibility to participate in that work in the world and preserve the quality, quantity, and availability of water for the world. We have already seen this failure happen in baptisms that are barely a damp mop and that have permitted us to neglect our baptismal responsibilities, particularly our responsibility for water. When the outcome is that the only water we know is so polluted as to be deadly, and we have long since gone to sonic showers, what of baptism? How can we bring life-giving water to a thirsty world if we do not know what that water looks, feels, acts, or tastes like?

Indeed, this is the third way a symbol can fail—through loss of the tactile dimension. When we cannot feel the weight of the bread in our hand or its texture on our tongue; when we cannot get our teeth around it and feel the momentary resistance and then the giving way, if we cannot taste it, how shall we know it is bread? How shall we know it is the bread of life? Only because we are told? But then symbol is reduced to something talked about rather than something experienced, and the most we will do to bring an end to poverty is talk about bringing an end to poverty rather than building a just society in fact.

Finally, a symbol may become dysfunctional because it no longer retains the connection between the past, the future, and our world here and now. The meal *is* a continuation of the earthly meals Jesus shared with friends and strangers—yet is *not* a repetition of them; it *is* the *present* reality of the future, eschatological banquet, but it is *not* the ultimate banquet. When we lose the balance between these dimensions of sharing meals at Christ's table, we reduce *cum panis,* communion, to medieval magic or to an empty ritual disconnected with actual eating and drinking and the satisfying of real hunger and thirst.

Living with Symbol

Even if we think we are not a symbolic people, if we intentionally eschew designs, paintings, banners, sculptures, we delude ourselves. Even a bare room is a symbol, speaking/embodying what it is not as much as what it is. If we leave a Bible open on the table or pulpit in the church, if we shape our building with a tall steeple or skylight over the chancel, if we are unwilling to change the hour of our weekly worship events, or attach a meal for street people to our worship event, we are engaging in symbolic as well as literal activity. So, as with all other aspects of our worship life, part of our ongoing conversation as a community of faith needs to swirl around the symbolic dimensions of our identity and our gathering. In the same way that the Reformers found the crucifix no longer able to serve gospel, might we now ask with people both inside and outside the church if the cross as an instrument of torture and death really bespeaks gospel now? Does our commitment to solidarity with the poor suggest we really ought to sell our silver communion service and replace it with humbler stuff? How can we most faithfully use water in baptism in a world sorely lacking in tender loving care of water and a world with too many places devastated by rampaging water? What do our pews really say about who we are?

Such questions will never stop if we are faithful people. We will always need to ask them anew for one reason alone: When we think that we have symbol figured out, when we think we have the place of the arts in worship defined, when we think we have gospel nailed, or God definitively named, when we think we have the answers in toto and for all time, people, and places, we delude ourselves. For what we are dealing with in word and music, in visual art and symbol is the God who *is* for us and with us in our ever-changing realities, and yet who is *not*, by any stretch of the imagination nor the most astute cognition, fully comprehensible. "For now we see in a mirror dimly, but then face to face. Now we know in part; then we shall understand fully, even as we have been fully understood" (1 Corinthians 13:12).

PART V

Building
Worship Events
from the Ground Up

CHAPTER 13

The Integrality of Worship

Throughout this book, we have been looking toward the enrichment of our worship life by considering worship events in terms of ideas, images, experiences, processes. We have been exploring aspects of worship one by one, picking them up and turning them over and inside out, and placing them in a different light in a different framework. Now, we begin to think about gathering up these aspects and putting them to work for us.

We know from the chapter on language that words can exert extraordinary power. The very words we use to describe and discuss worship and worship event components can help or hinder us as we take this next step in worshiping faithfully. Indeed, it was my own dissatisfaction with conventional definitions of "worship"[1] along with numerous experiences of "worship" that stopped at 12 noon just inside the sanctuary door that led me to rethink worship and define it as "life lived out in loving, dialogical relationship with God and all creation." This definition has been operating throughout the book, along with the recognition that in addition to worship writ large, we participate in particular worship events, microcosmic examples of the worship macrocosm.

Conventional definitions of worship are not the only words about worship that generate restlessness in me. I am also troubled by other words we use in relationship to worship, particularly preaching, or homiletics and liturgy, or preaching and worship.[2] We usually mean by the former

---

[1] One good collection of these can be found in James F. White, *Introduction to Christian Worship,* 31–36.

[2] All these terms carry a wide variety of meanings and usages—see White, *Introduction.* Some scholars distinguish between preaching homilies and preaching sermons, but in

the reading of scripture and speaking a sermon; by the latter, everything else that happens: prayer, hymnody, bath or meal, confession of sin or of faith, benediction, exchange of peace, etc.

The academic world generally sees worship/liturgy and preaching as two distinct disciplines. We maintain separate professional associations, and while each group may attend to the other discipline, it is clear where each group's real interest lies. The same distinction is evident in the classroom as well, where curricula usually separate preaching and liturgy/worship into distinct compartments, teaching one but not the other; or elevating one discipline to the lofty status of "required" while leaving the other an ambiguous "elective." Preaching classes may be taught as if Sundays were made for sermons not sermons for Sundays, and worship courses may be designed as if preaching is at best a poor second cousin of worship/liturgy or without considering preaching at all.

Not surprisingly, plenty of evidence of such a split abounds in the sanctuary, too. In some communities, we can see worship/liturgies scintillate and sparkle, but preaching is a lost art. Elsewhere, sermons reign supreme, and what precedes preaching is dismissed as "the preliminaries," and the community rarely gathers around the table of Christ. In many communities, the whole worship event is rarely prepared for with the same degree of care given to the preparation of sermons. Such services easily lack cohesiveness, and not infrequently does the theology of the sermon contradict that of the rest of the service. What then are we supposed to believe? do? In most communities as well, little attention is given to the fact that lectionaries we use in preaching have been drawn up to address liturgical interests, leaving preachers and communities to struggle with texts that "will not preach."[3]

We can celebrate a resurgence of interest in preaching in traditions where the discipline has suffered neglect and in worship/liturgy where it has had insufficient address. At the same time, we are still struggling to understand the relationship between the two. Listen to our language! We talk about Word *and* Sacrament or service of the word *and* service of the table as if they were two entirely different things.[4] We talk about preaching

---

either case may include everything from exhortation to storytelling. Liturgy, meaning "the work of the people," has its origins in civil, not ecclesial activity. Similarly, this term has been understood to apply to liturgical rites in printed form as often as to the acts of a community. Yet even additional usages and meanings are possible with these terms.

[3] Eugene L. Lowry, *Living With the Lectionary*, 1ff.

[4] Augustine says *Accedit verbum ad elementum et fit sacramentum.* "The Word is added to the element, and there results the sacrament." *A Select Library of The Nicene and Post Nicene Fathers of the Christian Church,* Vol. 7. Philip Schaff, ed., tr. John Gibb and James Innes (Edinburgh: T&T Clark; Grand Rapids: Eerdmans Publishing Co). *Joh. Tract.* 80.3. While

and worship, as if preaching were not an act of worship and worship not proclamation of gospel. We even speak of the sermon as God's word to us and worship/liturgy as our response to God. That ought to trouble us, given the Reformed tradition's insistence that all of worship is first and foremost God's gift to us.

Word=Act; Act=Word

True, most of Protestantism has long asserted the primacy of Word—because God *said* "let there be" and it was so, because the prophets were the *mouth* of God, because Christ Jesus is the *Word* of God who by parables and prayers discloses God to those who *hear*. But we know Word does not stand alone. God speaks and creation happens, indicating clearly that word and deed are one. Exodus claims that God *labors to* liberate the oppressed, that God moves with God's people through the wilderness in presence as visible as fire and cloud; that God feeds, waters and heals. Jeremiah confirms that we live because God *acts* in shaping our lives. God sends a fish to Jonah and grows a plant. Repeatedly the Older Testament insists on God's *active* presence with us.[5] Nor does Jesus, embodier of God *par excellence,* only preach and teach in parable, discourse, and prayer. In eating and drinking with Jesus, tax collectors and other "disreputable" guests recognized the presence of God—not because of what Jesus *said,* some suggest, but in sharing bread with the unacceptable—by what Jesus *did.* The Newer Testament affirms that we live ultimately because God reaches out to embrace us in the divine arms, claims us for life with God through Christ. The whole of scripture presents multiple visions of God making the divine self available to us—sometimes in precise, unarguable words: "You shall love your God with all your heart and your neighbor as yourself"; sometimes in ways too deep for words—fish and bread shared among 5,000 strangers. In commandment and flame, parable and meal, visible, physical touch and unknown nooks and crannies of the heart, mind, and soul, the Wisdom of God is spoken, done, and received, and we experience God's active love. Likewise, hymn, prayer, movement, sermon, table gathering, creed, silence, and waterworks *all* are media in which God may this day, this worship event, choose to act, meet, invite, call and command, to comfort, heal and free, to guide and to challenge—and not necessarily in that order.

---

concern here has to do with the words attached directly to the element, getting those words well said was hardly sufficient for Luther and Calvin, for whom, as we know, preaching in conjunction with the meal or bath was paramount.

[5] Samuel Terrien, *The Elusive Presence: The Heart of Biblical Theology* (San Francisco: Harper & Row, Pub., 1978).

Preaching thus is an *act* by which God proclaims and effects the grace of loving relationship—so also are prayer, song, silence, and stillness. But then, too, the meal is a word made visible, taste-able, a word textured, aromatic. Music pounds in our veins, or caresses our ears, taps our toes. Prayer weeps and shakes with laughter, clenches fists and loosens tongues. Silence, that oft-forgotten gift, gentles us to rest or sets us a-fidget or on fire as well as any collection of words. In words that *are* deeds, in *acts* that *proclaim* as clearly as any prophet's oracle, God engages with us and we discover the freedom to dart out a hand to touch for the barest second the hem of a robe or to make a 180 degree turnabout in the middle of a Damascus road.

Even when words are merely spoken, they are not *merely* spoken because speaking itself is an act with the potential to affect and effect. Tell me often that I am worthless and I may well muddle through life with shoulders hunched and eyes glued to the ground and never be of use to anyone. How much more the word of God not only says but does, transforming, when received in faith, not only attitudes and thought processes, but also behavior. Tell me often that God loves me and invites me to grow into fullness of life and to contribute to being in relationship with God and family, and I may well bring warm smiles and hot food to hungry, rejected people.

The same is true in reverse. The accident victim bleeds to death while we debate the merits and demerits of pressure pads versus tourniquets, but in the stopping of hemorrhage all the words are said before a mouth ever opens. Similarly hugs and handshakes, tears coursing down one's face or silent shaking laughter. We do not need verbiage to understand two people running to each other with arms held out amidst the bustle of an airport concourse. Pictures speak a thousand words. All the more, then, does bread held out to the hungry proclaim volumes.

Wholeness

Life is neither simple nor separable into distinct compartments. We do not live life as points on a line. We are not simply intellects or bodies; our souls do not exist independent of our thumbs and our cerebellums. We are, and do, in depth and in multiple dimensions all at once. You carry your toothache with you when you leave the house, and your tongue caresses that tooth through class or work and conversation all day long. What you are thinking shapes your posture, and your eyes and gestures mirror your thoughts perhaps more clearly than the words you utter. Likewise, when you fall in love, you do not hang your heart about the neck of your beloved while you go elsewhere to attend to your business!

Our realities are complex and multifaceted, and word, deed, sensation, and affect all shape our reality.

So, while John Calvin suggests that God accommodates Godself to us by providing material as means for us to encounter and be confirmed in the Compassionate One's loving embrace, he doesn't go far enough. If incarnation means anything, it means that God is fully present with us in the wholeness, the integrality of human being: mumbly mouth, fumbly feet and all. God recognizes full humanity not as a dualism of mind and body, word and deed, nor even as the two sides of a coin, but as an *integrality* that refuses to permit dichotomies and separate, even-if-parallel-or-equal constructions. To claim the primacy of word over deed or deed over word, to address either as if the other did not exist or were not really relevant manifests schizophrenia—divorce from reality.[6] This denies the very reality Christ Jesus proclaimed/did—that God indwells our very being, acting/speaking with us to make us whole, that we might speak/act with others to God's glory.

Worship as Multidirectional, Multidimensional Matrix

Another evidence of schizophrenia appears when a sermon is perceived as a "message," God's address to us, and the meal and everything else as our response (or more particularly, our *eucharistia*) to God.[7] Scripture gives us multiple affirmations that God does not engage us only in sermon and scripture, nor receive our response only in hymn and "sacrament." How long shall we try to box up our loving, bending-over-backward-for-us God like so many UPS packages? Would we preach at all if God were not at work in our hearts and minds, our knees and elbows, our mouths and ears? Nor would we sing if God did not sing with us the song; there would be no bath, meal, or anything else. Yet, God does not drag limp bodies and passive minds about the dance floor, but urges us to step into the divine choreography and to enter fully into the spirit of the movement. God invites us to be full members of the body of

---

[6] *Webster's Ninth New Collegiate Dictionary* (Springfield, Mass.: Merriam-Webster Inc., Publishers, 1983).

[7] See, for example, Reginald H. Fuller, *What is Liturgical Preaching?* (London: SCM Press, 1957), 10; William Willimon, *Preaching and Leading Worship* (Philadelphia: Westminster, 1984); Thomas H. Keir, *The Word in Worship: Preaching and its Setting in Common Worship* (London: Oxford University Press 1962); James F. White, *Sacraments as God's Self Giving* (Nashville: Abingdon Press, 1983), 64. Alternately, see William Skudlarek, *The Word in Worship: Preaching in a Liturgical Context* (Nashville: Abingdon Press, 1981), 69–71; Paul Hoon, *The Integrity of Worship* (Nashville: Abingdon Press, 1971) 107ff. More recent texts begin to move in a different direction, e.g., Mary Catherine Hilkert, *Naming Grace: Preaching and the Sacramental Imagination* (New York: Continuum, 1997), and Laurence Hull Stookey, *Eucharist: Christ's Feast with the Church* (Nashville: Abingdon Press, 1993).

Christ; full partners (*synergos*) in this embodiment of relationships of God with us and us with God-and-family.

So, worship events embrace multidimensional traffic, but there are no neat divisions marked by center lines and median strips. Nor do red and green traffic lights control the flow, now letting God "go" while we wait, then letting us "go" while God waits. Preaching/worship is organic, life happening all at once in all directions—all the while (by God's grace and our hard work) maintaining decency and order in function. Worship is deep weaving, a matrix the size of the cosmos, an ecosystem disordered only when we get our priorities out of place and time. It is not God toward us in sermon and us toward God in Supper; it is not that God approaches us in scripture and preaching and we respond in hymn or prayer, bath or meal. Who knows how God this day will dance and sing among us? Rather, worship enacts God—Emmanuel—*with* us in Word and deed, song and dance, bath and meal; it bespeaks us *with* God in Word and deed, song and dance, bath and meal—and not necessarily in that order. Trusting ultimately in God to enliven us, we nonetheless do all our homework, tuning our whole selves to peak participation levels, giving as much attention to planning the hymns, offering, prayer, greeting, and meal as we give to the sermon. We are engaging, after all, in a *dialogue*, *wholistic* dialogue.

The Fullness of Sacrament

We might consider that bath and meal reveal particularly powerfully the integrality of worship. Unless we are willing to surrender to Pelagius,[8] we must admit these elements are, like everything else in worship, always God's act of love with us. By nature they proclaim—because they announce the gospel of God, precisely as they body it forth as they incarnate God's love for us. But by virtue of our activity of physically carrying out bath and meal, God effects this disclosure, this presence, this communion through and with human beings. Holy Presence is particularized as each of us tastes and swallows the food and drink from the table or feels baptismal water running down. Indeed, the same is equally true of preaching: Those who preach body forth God's love,[9] for who could preach apart from love? Who could hear apart from allowing sound waves to connect through eardrums and the nervous system with gray matter, memories, and imagination? Then preaching is also sacrament? Yes, as are singing a hymn, exchanging peace, and praying for others.

---

[8] Pelagius was deemed a heretic for insisting humankind can take initial steps toward God, rather than being dependent on God's prevenient grace and moving first toward us.

[9] See *A Kinesthetic Homiletic: Embodying Gospel in Preaching.*

We deceive ourselves if we see sacramental events primarily as our response of faith and/or thanks to God, as our service to God, or as anything other than profound love spoken, profound proclamation bodied forth to us and participated in by us in touch, taste, movement, and yes, sound, and silence. Worship is integrated activity, body and soul, mind and heart, emotion and reason, inhale/exhale, contract/release—all interacting in multidimensions all at once. Each moment gathers up an occasion of God and us engaging together in living in loving, dialogical relationship. Perhaps we should return to speaking of worship as "Holy Communion," and not just on those occasions where the breaking of bread occurs.

Worship: Work of People and Pastor Together, Start to Finish

We are dealing here with an organic whole, indeed, with an ecosystem. The whole of worship has to do with gospel: with the love of God for us and us for God and neighbor, with loving, dialogical, multidimensional relationship, with nothing less than the living, organic family of God.

Yet, here we too often see another schism: the one between clergy and laity, the one that says pastors are solely responsible for sermons and for presiding, even if they permit the people a hand in the liturgy. If gospel belongs to everyone, if worship constitutes a whole, an ecosystem, if worship events embody dialogical relationship, responsibility for preaching cannot belong to pastors alone, any more than liturgy can be the work of the people if they are merely passive users of someone else's design rather than codesigners and coembodiers of it, from start to finish.

We need to let go the notion that preachers prepare a sermon *for* the congregation and deliver it *to* them. We need to begin to think in terms of preachers creating sermons *with* the folk in the pew. So also presiders and worship leaders need to surrender the conviction they are called to design and do worship events *for* the congregation and recognize they design and do worship *with* the congregation. A congregation's ownership of worship and preaching cannot begin only after the sermon is prepared and the prayers designed.

If we take seriously the integrality of worship and the baptismal claim that we are all members of the body, the entire preparation for and development of worship events will move out of the confines of the study into intentional, grassroots involvement in the whole life of the congregation.

Those who have designated responsibilities for the worship life of the church face an awesome task. It may not be the task we thought it was— finding the magic form, the perfect style, the exact gesture, the irresistible words to present to "our" people. It is, rather, the task of surrendering insistence on compartmentalizing—of keeping everything in its place: sermon here, liturgy there, pastor in the pulpit, people in the pew, worship in the sanctuary, life in the world. Rather, worship leaders have the task of integrating, of healing, making whole, the worship of the church. This can be helped by inviting many people in a congregation to share in the experience of engaging with scripture from the ground up, of coming to the experience of embodying gospel from the inside out rather than simply trying on an already "finished" product.

Perhaps this week the youth group will work with more trained leaders to shape the sermon and compose prayers or hymns. Perhaps next week the building committee will wrestle with the text and together with pastor, musician, and others will construct a new worship order. Perhaps instead of fading away after they have formally joined, the new member class will meet regularly for the next year and with pastoral staff work out four or six or eight whole worship events to be shared by the whole community. And the seniors hot-meals group, the education committee, the AIDS support group and the fourth-grade Sunday school class, and maybe even the Out-of-the-Cold participants. Worship is our whole life in dialogue with God and each other, but how will it be so if we do not build in the life of the whole body and experience together the life of faith?

Radically Integrated Worship

What God offers and we need is the experience of the ecosystem of God. Jesus' own ministry makes plain that God is *with* us, and that the fullness and wholeness of life with God are meant to shape and power our Christian being as individuals and our gatherings for worship here and now.

Thus we must question all the processes we use in developing and experiencing worship events, and we must question the language about worship that we use, even the language I use in this volume. If we are serious about incorporating preaching, then preaching will be liturgy— the people's work. If hymn, prayer, meal, and all those things categorized under the term liturgy also proclaim gospel, preaching will describe them. But perhaps these very words are bankrupt. If so, what language can we find or create that will more fully reveal the integrated character of what we have until now called worship/liturgy and preaching? How can we more faithfully honor in language this fluid engagement of loving God with us and us with God and each other?

Together we share the burden and the privilege of helping to bring the church alive through worship that is pervasive, whole, organic. But we do not bear it alone. God empowers us for this radically integrated worship because worship is God's gift with us; because word done and deed said are God's act and become our response; because worship, ordained ministry and the ministry of the whole people of God are of a piece with organic, integrated, and multidimensional life in the family of God. Perhaps the language will arise from the experience as clergy increasingly surrender claims to fame and power, authority and privilege to become coworkers with the folk in the pew, enabling them to take their rightful place in the research, design, and development of whole worship events.

The stuff of worship is the stuff of life with God-and-family, all of it; the stuff of worship is the body of Christ, ear, toe, artery, pancreas. This life does not occur in discrete steps from study to chancel, chancel to pew, pew to home, home to street. It occurs all at once, surrounded by and intermixed with the whole people of God, in the street at the same time as in the church building, in the study at the same time as in the kitchen, in the classroom at the same time as in the marketplace. Perhaps, if we begin to create worship events this way, we will more truly and fully live worshipful lives, and the world may begin to breathe again.

CHAPTER 14

Collaborators in Creation

When I was a child, I did the same thing every Sunday morning in church. Very little changed from week to week, except on those rare occasions when the congregation celebrated communion and the service took somewhat longer than usual. Everything to be done in either case was set down in a book, and although hymns, sermons, and some prayers varied, after a while they all began to sound the same. Apart from my joy of singing, I remember being utterly bored because in all the dramatic changes I encountered in myself and my world as I grew up, I was always treated in church as if I had not changed at all.

I found Sunday mornings as a Presbyterian pastor not a whole lot different, except that I was much more invested by virtue of being responsible. The Session defined our pattern of worship. I could vary from it only with their express permission, and they didn't give it very often. So Sunday after Sunday we did the same things, even though there were volcanoes rumbling in the basement of the congregation's life, and the world in which we lived was not in the same place this week as it was last week.

As a doctoral student I enjoyed more Sunday morning freedom than ever before. The opportunity to visit different faith communities offered the hope of diversity in worship experiences that could perhaps refresh me through difference if not address me where I had come to be in life just then. Difference at least kept me on my toes. And yet, so often I went away feeling I'd been in a time warp, that nothing had happened that had anything to do with the realities in which everyone present lived. I put it down to the paralysis of the familiar, the numbing comfort of the old shoe that held congregations in thrall doing what they had always done by habit, such that even if what they did was somewhat different for me because it was new to me, it wasn't different for them, and it wasn't addressing them where they really lived. Sunday morning was an opportunity for memories, reminiscences, and for amnesia about now.

"Convergence"

In recent years we have seen developing among many Christian denominations an amazing concurrence about the nature and practice of worship, including a healthier balance between addressing the intellect and attending to the whole person and community. This is all to the good since gospel has to do with whole persons and manifests itself in both cognitive and embodied ways. To neglect either of those dimensions leaves us mired in superstitious ritual or abstract concepts and dishonors Jesus the Christ, who both ate and talked with those around him. However, this consensus also manifests itself in an apparent drive to make normative a particularly defined order of service. Readers can see this pattern in most recently published denominational worship books and contained within it, a specific, standardized meal prayer that generally follows that of the so-called Apostolic Tradition of Hippolytus and its descendants.

At least part of the rationale behind this push toward homogeneity in worship is the laudable desire to enhance the unity of the church. Yet I find more and more disquieting the notion that a singular, routinized pattern of worship or prayer can be truly life-giving for both regular gatherings of a given community and for the worship events of communities that are specially gathered. Other voices now join me in my concern. In the first place, the notion that there is a singular, normative profile of worship evidenced within Christian history cannot be sustained.[1] Along with that, we increasingly recognize that worship events need to engage in responsible conversation with particular cultures and faith communities.[2] James White has written, "Perhaps we should do more to encourage diversity rather than to seek consensus. We do not yet have enough varieties of Christian worship."[3] Amen to that! Further, Stephen Farris

---

[1] Allan Bouley, *From Freedom to Formula* (Washington: Catholic University of America Press, 1981). See also Bradshaw, *The Search for the Origins of Christian Worship.*

[2] Anscar J. Chupungco, OSB, *Liturgies of the Future: The Process and Methods of Inculturation,* (New York: Paulist Press, 1989) and *Liturgical Inculturation: Sacramentals, Religiosity, and Catechesis* (Collegeville: The Liturgical Press, 1992); Kevin J. Irwin, *Context and Text: Method in Liturgical Theology* (Collegeville: Pueblo, 1994); David N. Power, *Worship: Culture & Theology* (Washington: The Pastoral Press., 1990), 277. For a homiletical perspective, see Leonora Tubbs Tisdale, *Preaching as Local Theology and Folk Art* (Minneapolis: Fortress Press, 1997).

[3] James F. White, *A Brief History of Christian Worship* (Nashville: Abingdon Press, 1993), 179.

has echoed these thoughts: "…uniformity in the Christian church is neither possible nor desirable. We ought to know by now that attempts to impose uniformity paradoxically end up damaging the unity we should seek. The earliest image of the church is that of the body of Christ, an image that fully allows for and even demands diversity."[4] He also takes issue with the use of worship patterns rooted in the third and fourth centuries. From his perspective, the worship of this period is "too late" in terms of having already abandoned the radical acts of Jesus and the earliest Christian communities regarding world view, relations with God and others, faithful worship, and so forth.[5] We need our memories, no doubt. But how shall we use them

Feminist scholarship has also addressed problems with worship reform rooted in traditions of the past.[6] Not only has worship content been androcentrically constructed, but to the degree content and form are inseparable, we must also admit to the likely androcentric character of the forms. Even apart from that, as far as these worship patterns have *failed* to obliterate sexism, racism, handicappism, etc., we must ask why any church that understands the link between worship and justice would continue to perpetuate injustice by normalizing a worship praxis rooted in the unjust past. What "authority" could possibly justify that?[7]

The Constancy of Change

Many churches' efforts to expand language in response to feminist theological claims reflect the fact that we *are* in the midst of a paradigm shift. But a paradigm shift requires more than a move toward more inclusive language. This is especially so because we live in and are called to embody gospel in a world that is changing faster than we can grasp. Every

---

[4] Stephen Farris, "Reformed Identity and Reformed Worship," in *Reformed World* (June, 1993), 70.

[5] Stephen Farris, "The New Testament, the Holy and Reformed Identity." *Encounter* 57/4, p. 325. See also "Reformed Identity," p. 74, in which Farris notes: The New Testament…blesses God, the third century consecrates elements…women took a much fuller role in worship than do their daughters of the third-century…The New Testament is profoundly anti-hierarchical; a hierarchy has emerged by the third century."

[6] See, for example, Marjorie Procter-Smith, *In Her Own Rite: Constructing Feminist Liturgical Tradition* (Nashville: Abingdon Press, 1990) and *Praying with Our Eyes Open: Engendering Feminist Liturgical Prayer* (Nashville: Abingdon Press, 1995).

[7] Nathan Mitchell, on the basis of Ron Grimes' work, has recently suggested that "ritual needs to be *divested* of…claims to authority" the likes of which have underwritten the value of making normative worship practice based on third and post-third century tradition. Nathan Mitchell, "The Amen Corner," *Worship* 67/1 (January 1993): 80.

day technology presents us with some new ethical issue; every day new political crises leave our global village gasping for fresh expressions of hope; every day our churches find themselves with emptier pews and emptier bank books with which to fund the mission of God. We need worship that not only comforts and supports us, but also that rouses from sleep the imagination we must exercise vigorously if we are to be able truly to love God and neighbor in our time and place.

Yet, my own experience with set liturgical texts as a child, with routinized worship orders, and now with the "consensus" effort convicts me that the normative use of such worship patterns leaves worshipers increasingly disconnected from concrete aspects of daily life, stifled theologically, numbed by sameness, and just plain bored. Even though worship events following the consensus pattern may contain gospel content, rarely do they provide adequate vision, experience or rehearsal of gospel, or exercise of imagination sufficient to enable me to meet the rapidly changing world in which I live. The emptiness of pews suggests I am not alone in this.

Some people seem to thrive on worship constancy. Even so, human beings are not homogeneous. People are constructed differently externally and internally. Some of us are introverts, others extroverts. Some of us love cold, dry weather, others hot, humid weather. Some of us are politically conservative, others radical. Some live as mystics, others as pragmatists. Some require consistency for spiritual and personal wholeness, while I and others like me require diversity. Most of us consist of a dynamic blend of such traits, a blend that may rove back and forth across a wide spectra. The effect of that is that there simply is not one right way to be human or even to be Christian. Nor is there one right way to worship God or to worship God as a Christian.[8]

Equally important is the fact that God is bigger than any single descriptor or any related set of descriptors. So also, God transcends any particular style or pattern of worship or prayer can manifest. Therefore, if we claim or behave as if there is a normative way to worship, we not only

---

[8] Luther and Calvin insisted that consciences not be burdened by requirements that were not scriptural—else we engage in works righteousness. They were conscientious about claiming that their orders of worship, as well as the texts that were contained in them, were models—not mandates. Some traditions refused models altogether, and thus worship directories came into use, outlining principles to be followed, but not providing either pattern or content, lest pattern or content be identified as norm or mandate. See Carol Doran and Thomas H. Troeger, *Trouble at the Table: Gathering the Tribes for Worship* (Nashville: Abingdon Press, 1992) for a useful exposition of the nonhomogeneous character of congregations, along with some strategies for developing a congregationally based worship life.

deny human diversity and the variety of human reality, but we also attempt again to put *God* in a box by limiting the way we are to relate with God and therein the way we expect God to relate with us. Thus we "worship" one we have defined rather than the One Who Is/Will Be, the One who was revealed by Jesus of Nazareth to engage with human beings quite often in surprising, *ab*normal ways, but clearly in ways that met individuals in their particularity.

If, as Calvin saw it, God continually accommodates the divine self to human capacity, while God *might* relate with us in the same ways God did in the past, God *will* relate with us *in our particularity*. As that changes, we may understand that God's engagement with us may also change. To attempt to engage in worship in a singular form such as the consensus model, let alone a form molded by antiquity seems to offer little hope that our worship life will honor God's and our interaction in the uniquenesses of our late-twentieth-century contexts, or that we will effectively embody gospel in circumstances radically removed from earlier contexts.

I value conserving that which is good within the worship traditions of Christianity. After all, although I once evicted the church from my life, we have long observed a reconciliation, if a somewhat restless one. That is because I am perhaps foolishly convinced that more than any other arena of human life, the church is most likely to be about the business of gospel—even if it often manifests itself in conventional ways. At the very least, I can always call the church to be accountable to gospel. More, I do not wish to lose my memories, to be stripped of conscious, internal awareness of all that has gone into making me who I am. One blotted-out year of my life is enough to disinterest me in total amnesia. That we know so little of the history of Christianity-at-worship, particularly in the early years and particularly with regard to women, is disastrous enough. The real question, then, is not *whether* we conserve, but *what* we conserve and *how.*

My answer to that is not form and/or content nor routinized process, but gospel. True, gospel is not a simple matter. Not everyone will agree with my definition of gospel: the event of God loving us and engaging with us in dialogical relationship. But even if they do, God comes to us with love where *we* are, not where someone else is or once was. That means fluidity and honoring diversity of context and persons are inherent to gospel. So it should not surprise us that scripture does not show us a singular, normative pattern of theology or worship, let alone one that is good for all times and places. Reading scripture, examining tradition, describing gospel and worship itself are always interpretive endeavors, because *subjectively* speaking, at least, gospel changes in expression and manifestation.[9]

We can remain open to such gospel dynamism as intrinsic to worship events if we adopt as our operating principle the claim of this volume, that worship events are microcosmic experiences of engaging in loving, dialogical relation with God and neighbor. If that is the character of the whole event, then the very way we structure the event needs to speak that same reality.

Four Approaches

In the face of all this, how do we enable people to worship authentically? Given the opportunity to design worship events, where does one begin? I identify four possible approaches to constructing worship events. The first I call the "What other folks have done" approach. Here congregations/denominations adopt (or adapt), for example, the pattern Justin describes (gathering, readings, homily, prayers, meal); the pattern of the so-called eucharistic prayer of Hippolytus; or fourth-century patterns such as that of baptism as an extended initiation rite. Many congregations have absorbed the Reformation emphasis on preaching with the resulting domination of the oral/aural to the neglect of full embodiment of gospel, including gathering about the table. Others may take up what the church the next town over does—like putting an anthem between scripture and sermon or adding a children's sermon. Or they may simply opt for a wholesale appropriation of the "consensus" pattern printed in new denominational books. This approach can maintain a sense of solidarity with the past. It can also produce worship events that have little connection with contemporary realities.

The second approach I call the "laundry list" approach. It is often based on the notion that you can't have a worship service without a couple of hymns, scripture, prayers, etc. Conversely, items may disappear, sometimes for no evident reason. Often there is no apparent rhythm or purpose—either practical or theological—in the placement of the items, and theological coherence and flow may be lacking. Yet this manner of shaping worship may leave more room for the movement of the Spirit than those that present a fixed content.

The third approach is the "scriptural pattern" approach—constructing worship events on the basis of Isaiah 6, for example, with its pattern of praise, confession of sin, declaration of pardon, call, proclamation. The

---

[9] See my article "Worship as Hermeneutic: Interpreter of the Gospel," *Consensus* 16/1 (1990): 27–44.

merit of this approach rests on its scriptural foundation. There aren't any worship blueprints in scripture, however, and even if there were, they wouldn't necessarily be appropriate to this time and place. Yet as suggested above, this can be true of all these approaches although any of these patterns *may* help particular congregations engage faithfully in the worship enterprise, in loving dialogical relationship with God and neighbor. My experience with these patterns, along with conversations with many others who have encountered them, raises a serious question about how adequately these approaches *do* empower faithful worship in our current global living.

We will take up the fourth approach shortly, but first let us consider some foundational ideas. Every worship event enacts a theological claim of some sort or other, for better or worse. The *order* in which we do things, the *content* we include, and the *process* we use in arriving at that can manifest, for example, that God is welcoming or hostile, emotional or intellectual, dynamic or static. People may discover themselves to be embraced, repudiated, empowered, disempowered, or just plain confused. Order can enhance the content or contradict it; together with process they can embody gospel or disembody and eviscerate it.

Thus, intentionality with regard to order as well as content is essential. So, for example, some congregations of the Disciples of Christ put the meal at the beginning of the service. Why? Because they understand unmediated experience of the gift of the meal to be the best possible way of welcoming people into encounter and dialogue with Christ. Only after such encounter, they believe, is it possible for people to proclaim Christ, to pray, to praise God, to commit to Christ's ministry, to live lovingly. Most other Christian communities put the meal after the sermon. They understand with the Reformers that we can do without everything but the Word, and that there would be no communion without the word of promise. Some also see the meal as incarnating or responding to the preached word, and their logic suggests that is possible only *after* the word is preached.

Keeping in mind that gospel is God relating with us in our time and place, the question to ask is, "What makes theological sense, *gospel* sense, for this community here and now?"

Designing Worship Events as Gospel Experience

Since gospel is intimately connected with scripture, corporate Christian worship life requires congregational engagement with scripture. Gospel is also relational, having to do with how we relate with God and one another. Therefore, at least three sources or texts interact together as partners in creating the worship experience:

1. tradition (inclusive of scriptural, extracanonical, theological, and liturgical resources);

2. particular community (inclusive of preacher-presider, congregation, and immediate ecclesially and societally related bodies);

3. cosmic reality (including the vast diversity and complexity of our global home and its peoples, as well as its extraterrestrial context).

Each multidimensional source or text inherently and dynamically interrelates with the others. None of them automatically can claim priority or primacy over the others, if we believe/experience that God *is* God-with-us, deeply invested in and manifested in each "text," as are we. God, then, partners us, at least as the context in which we all live and have our being, as the primary *dynamis* or power that fuels the entire process,[10] and as the live-in partner in everyone's whole life.

Nevertheless, in each text we are hard pressed to find gospel *all* the time. For instance, in scripture, we may rightly question whether gospel can now be found in the sacrifice of Jephthah's daughter or Paul's advice to Philemon. As well, reformers of every persuasion have found valid reason to suggest that worship has from time to time gone astray, including that of the reformers themselves. Even if our communities revel in gospel Sunday after Sunday, do they embody gospel if they do not do so with the rest of the world? Could a tradition so radically exclusive be "orthodox," engaged in right praise? Liberation theologians have helped us see gospel wherever in the world people lovingly feed the hungry and champion freedom of the oppressed, and we have consistently spoken of God revealed in nature. Still, our cosmic text is ambivalent as any other concerning social relating and nature's expression. We may sometimes find gospel on the "underside" of particular texts, i.e., where gospel is *not*.[11] In any case, each source proffers gospel only in relation to the others, as unique gift, supplement, corrective. None does so independently of the others, any more than the fingers are independent of the stomach or the spinal column and vice versa.

---

[10] Creation theology, humanity as *imago dei* and the temple of the Spirit, scripture as God-inspired, and so on, to say nothing of ecosystemic theories and scientific notions of matter-energy continua and the like, all support such ideas. Helpful resources include Sallie McFague's *The Body of God: An Ecological Theology* (Minneapolis: Fortress Press, 1993) and Peter C. Hodgson's *Winds of the Spirit: A Constructive Christian Theology* (Louisville: Westminster/John Knox Press, 1994). His discussion of hermeneutics is particularly helpful, but the entire volume is important for moving worship into the next century, although Hodgson's own discussion of this particular concern is less than inspired.

[11] Paul S. Wilson, *Imagination of the Heart: New Understandings in Preaching* (Nashville: Abingdon Press, 1988), 109ff; and, *The Practice of Preaching* (Nashville: Abingdon Press, 1995), chap. 2.

We live, then, in a dynamic, multihued matrix in constant transformation. We cannot normalize or canonize our reality except in the constancy of constant change. We do not have immutable canonical texts or forms, but partners in dialogue in the dance of life in relationship that seeks to engage in an ongoing exchange of love for the sake of the whole. Worship itself is that ongoing reality, and Sunday morning events find their purpose as a microcosm of that ongoing gospel. Participants ought to be able to count on gospel being profoundly embodied in these gatherings, not only for the sake of those present, but for the sake of the whole cosmos.

Attempting to accomplish this with essentially static forms, groups, or processes is inconsistent with the dynamism of gospel and human life. Consequently, I propose that we engage various "members" of each "text" in multidimensional conversation/choreography toward the end of creating together worship events that are as wholistic and alive an interweaving of our partners as we, together with God, can manage.

Step-by-Step

One way of pursuing this adventure is by following this or a similar procedure.

1. Gather from the congregation a group with as wide a representation as possible well in advance of the event date to engage in the planning process.

2. Agree on a text from tradition (including scripture), community, or globe on which to focus.

3. Engage in an imaginative, whole-being process of exploring the focal text. This may be begun with a deep breathing exercise such as begins chapter 4 and proceed with explorations in movement, arts, and conversation.[12]

4. Include in the engagement with the focal text other aspects of tradition, community, globe by asking how they relate with one another e.g., what in the life of the community, in tradition, in the cosmos already embodies content discovered in the focal text or fails to do so?

5. Decide what experience of gospel the texts in partnership can provide the larger community. It may be helpful to frame the gospel experience in a simple verbal or movement sentence.

---

[12] I describe an embodied approach in my book, *A Kinesthetic Homiletic.* A more cerebral method is described in John S. McClure, *The Round-table Pulpit: Where Leadership and Preaching Meet* (Nashville: Abingdon Press, 1995).

6. Agree on the means of sharing the gospel experience, e.g., with a central focal point such as a sermon, mime, or litany; with several focal points with equal or varied intensity.

7. Work out how to help the community Gather into the chosen Gospel experience, and to Go out to share that experience of gospel with the rest of the world.

I have nicknamed this the "three-G" approach to ordering a worship event, since the elemental form of both the planning process and the worship event itself is Gathering, Gospel, and Going forth. Those three things need to happen in any worship event. The three g's do not, however, represent separate compartments, since we are always on the move, and gospel permeates our comings and goings, as well as our being in between. The structure does help keep the flow of the event moving, as it reminds us always to ask three questions: What is the key experience for the day? How do we gather people into it from wherever they have come? How do we help them move on?

Key Principles

When we plan worship in this manner, we do not impose the form or movement on the event beyond the unavoidable three-G structure. Rather the flow of the event arises from the intersection of text and people in their particularities. Note also that scripture readings do not govern the whole, *gospel* does. Lectionary use remains a flexible choice, and just because a hymn is listed somewhere as reflecting a chosen text doesn't mean it suits today. Rather, we seek out hymns that can enable this people to participate in the gospel event of this text today. So also we design and include other elements of prayer, silence, enactment in the manner that most prepares, enhances, or helps the congregation move into or on from the core gospel experience.

Because gospel funds the whole, gospel embraces all these people in their context, it is essential in shaping the service to care for congregational inclusivity. That means not only including congregational members in the entire planning process, but also attending to the congregation as *whole* beings—people who live by ear, eye, taste, and smell, movement and stillness, emotions as well as cognition and spirit. We need, as well, to remember also the evaluative process, because we are accountable to one another not only within the congregation but also in the world, present, past, and future. What advanced gospel? What didn't? What can we learn from this? What could we do differently that would enrich the worship life of our family both in the sanctuary and in the world?

These same premises/concerns apply no matter the type of service. If a funeral sets the context or a baptism, the basic process remains the same. Those compelled to use a set liturgical construct can also adapt the process for their use. They might ask, "How does the gospel experience affect this order?" and, "How can we help our congregation create and express their own gospel content?" Those who engage in deep dialogue with a text will surely be able to build a prayer of confession in concert with the text's gospel claims and the reality of their own community. They are also well-disposed to find hymns appropriate to the service as a whole and the people as a whole—with the help of the congregation's musicians.

The point is gospel calls us to think and act theologically together through *every* aspect of our worship events, existent worship order or no, no matter the liturgical season, no matter that "it has always been done this way." Worship events as gospel participate in ever-new relationship with God and others in ever-new circumstances. Gospel never sits on its *status quo* and neither can we.

Gifts of Change

I do not presume that this group-process design for creating worship anew around the gospel claim/experience of a particular day for a particular people will remedy all that is wrong with the church and/or its worship, that it will redeem Christianity from postmodern marginalization, or that it is free of problems. Some might see the time and energy commitment required of participants among the latter, although rarely do we give credence to this concern in the preaching endeavor. Lack of the benefits of continuity and neglect of the larger ecclesial context are also possible. Others might have concern for orthodoxy or aesthetics. But these considerations apply to any approach and can be addressed in ways other than by imposing set forms/texts.

Moreover, the benefits of designing worship in this way are multiple. In an age of epidemic biblical illiteracy, a community that chooses to use canonical scripture as the primary text of tradition can then root this process in contemporary, local, and active engagement of particular people with the Bible. People's encounter with the scripture moves much beyond hearing it read and preached on to exploring it themselves with all the resources, breadth, and depth theological schools aim to provide their students. The more people substantively engage and are engaged by biblical texts, the more fully and richly they will know scriptural content and find it a life-giving resource for the whole of their existence, individual and communal.

Theologically speaking, we can discern in the scheme a Trinitarian dimension. God *gathers* together and therein creates a people, God embraces them with *gospel* through Christ, and God empowers them by the Spirit to *go* and serve in the world at large. This Trinitarian event remains fully dialogical in that people actively participate in every phase of God's activity. Moreover, by creating worship texts afresh, we enhance the possibility of presenting much more of God than we can do when we use the same texts or even the same pattern of prayer or the same tightly defined order of worship. As well, we can enjoy freedom from the absurdity of trying to say/do everything every time. Preachers have long recognized the impossibility of preaching the whole gospel in every sermon. What we are about in worship is more than a single event or a single approach can bear.

This approach also can easily avoid the conflicts that may result when one person or group constructs the "liturgy" and another the sermon. Here a single group remains involved in the entire work from deciding on texts to worship design—including sermon development—to implementation of the whole. Yet, there is ample room to welcome tradition into the process, if only because as groups change, participants will ask questions arising from their own knowledge and experience of diverse worship traditions, questions of meaning, reason, and value for the present, questions that can in turn enrich participant knowledge of the tradition. Theological and worship imperialism will have considerably less room to grow in a medium that continually or even frequently changes.

As the process celebrates diverse theological and worship traditions, content, and interests, so also it celebrates the pastoral diversity of any community. Instead of generic texts expected to function universally but which, for that very reason, often lack depth and concreteness, specific, whole-body expressions of a particular community can be built into the event. That expands the possibilities that more people will connect with worship events more frequently. More important, as this corporate process enables participants to develop concrete skills in intersecting gospel with today's life, we have increased hope that people will be more able to live as Christians not just one hour per week but twenty-four hours per day, not just for their own or their congregation's sake, but in and for the whole world.

Even in a community where liturgical constancy is a need or a value, this approach to "putting worship together" for the day or the season is possible and can produce these many benefits. Simply by involving more and more people in a congregation in the work of sermon development and conversation about how each one relates to the worship of the day, we can encourage deeper investment in the worship event and rehearse one another for our worship life outside the sanctuary doors.

Gospel calls us to think and act theologically in *every* aspect of our worship—no matter whether there is an existent worship order, no matter what the season is, no matter that "it has always been done this way"— because gospel, as an event of relationship with God and neighbor, forms the heart out of which worship arises. For the same reason, gospel calls us to function corporately, communally, from start to finish. This design, experience reveals, produces theologically coherent, fully communal, gospel centered worship.

CHAPTER 15

Sampler

But "what does grace look like walking around?" In chapter 14, we explored a process of constructing worship events from the gospel out, from the ground up, from the inside out. But talking about that as an idea, in abstract, conceptual language is not the same thing as seeing it in living color, walking around.

With this chapter I hope to try to enable you to see grace walking around, to evoke in your imagination gospel as embodied in a worship event constructed according to the premises and processes we have already explored. Given the limited dimensions of a written text, I set out on a challenging task, perhaps an impossible one. Yet, I want to provide at least one example of what can result when this book is put into practice, not as a model or template, but in order to give you, my readers, a "through the glass darkly" video of what the kind of worship we have been considering might look like in fact. In order to do so, I rehearse the process involved in crafting the service and include a descriptive script and commentary of the worship event itself.

A script is not a worship event any more than any liturgical text is. A script does provide structure, content, and choreography, but participants do not necessarily render the text of a script "verbatim." As well, what a planning group intends doesn't always occur. An assembly is, after all, a living body that may choose to move differently than a script suggests. Moreover, life in the assembly is influenced by the unique character and contexts of that community in ways that cannot be drawn out here. Yet a script can provide significant clues to a moment of life, as can every liturgical, scriptural, historical, literary text, and it can open doors to the imagination and to new perceptions, understandings, and experiences.

Setting the Scene

Trinity St. Paul's United Church, located in central Toronto, is an unusually diverse and missionally immersed congregation. Participants in its worship life quickly become accustomed to and relish the constancy of change in worship events. The current pastor works both with a worship committee and weekly with a worship planning team. As well, other teams may be constituted for particular worship events, or various groups in the congregation may function as a planning team. The event attested to below was created by a team gathered by open invitation to prepare for a worship event I was responsible for in the pastor's absence.[1] In this case, meeting as we were over the summer, the team was extremely dynamic in its membership as participants came and went on holiday. As well, they represented important aspects of our congregation's diversity.

We began with a deep breathing exercise and a reading of texts proposed by the lectionary. The Ecclesiastes pericope was chosen as focal by the text of a congregation needing to deal with the pericope's issues and by the text of global community demonstrating insistent social injustice and trauma. As we explored the Ecclesiastes text through movement and allowed it to direct us, we together choreographed isolated, random, repetitive, nonproductive movement brought to a sudden halt in protest. A weaving together of individual circular movements into a single circle around a basket of luscious, spring fruits brought as a gift to us by one of the participants followed. We completed the "weaving" by gathering up the fruit and moving as a whole toward the street, expressing the desire and commitment to take nourishment to hungry street-dwellers. That choreography evoked an idea map of saying, doing, and experience statements:

What the text says: We have no power to influence the world.

What the text does: Challenges us to come to terms with this "truth."

What gospel experience will we share with the congregation: One of accepting and resisting this "truth," and then of cocreating the music of the universe.

We opted to express this gospel experience partly in a sermon and shaped the rest of the service by exploring how to bring the congregation into the sermon and where to go following it—the trinitarian, three-G pattern noted in the previous chapter. The event occurred on August 6, 1995, the ninth Sunday after Pentecost.

---

[1] Ann Stewart, Catherine Manning, Chris Rose, Gordon MacNeill, Laurence and Akeylah, Lynn Jondreville, Pamela Moeller, Sarah Yoon.

The Script	The Commentary
Organ Prelude	Because we wanted to affirm that this worship event grows out of the community as a whole, the team chose to have the worship leaders seat themselves in the pews rather than to process in after the congregation had assembled. At the appropriate times, each then took her or his place facing the community to lead the activity. The greeting, including a welcome and the naming of our purpose in gathering as worship, was offered extemporaneously. The location of announcements varies, as may all worship components at TSP. We chose this location as part of gathering and constituting ourselves as a part of a particular community engaged in diverse activities of ministry and concern. The choice of hymn served the same purpose. It specifically names our life of faith and our gathering for worship as shaped and fueled by God-with-us, thus affirming God's presence rather than "invoking" it.
Greeting, Announcements, and Concerns of the Community	
*Hymn: What is the Place²	

Organ Prelude

Because we wanted to affirm that this worship event grows out of the community as a whole, the team chose to have the worship leaders seat themselves in the pews rather than to process in after the congregation had assembled. At the appropriate times, each then took her or his place facing the community to lead the activity. The greeting, including a welcome and the naming of our purpose in gathering as worship, was offered extemporaneously. The location of announcements varies, as may all worship components at TSP. We chose this location as part of gathering and constituting ourselves as a part of a particular community engaged in diverse activities of ministry and concern. The choice of hymn served the same purpose. It specifically names our life of faith and our gathering for worship as shaped and fueled by God-with-us, thus affirming God's presence rather than "invoking" it.

Greeting, Announcements, and Concerns of the Community

*Hymn: What is the Place²

Gathering of the young/young at heart

This segment affirmed children as integral to the community at worship, and freed them to participate fully in the service or to gather at a table located in a corner of the worship space to read, color, or otherwise occupy themselves as suited to their age, disposition, and ability while yet remaining in the community. This day the children chose full participation. The father of two young children read a story of Anansi the Spider demonstrating the cooperative, life-giving work enacted in our worship.

Scripture I: Eccl. 1:12–18

Because the scripture reading launched the gospel core, we located it here to help the congregation move quickly into the gospel experiences it initiated. We read the last half of the lection *before* the centering exercise and the first half after, since in our experience in planning we found the second half to set the context and to deal with generalities that the first half particularized and emphasized.

Centering

As the worship planning team worked with these verses, we discovered that the Teacher was stuck in his head, functioning as a disembodied intellect. None of us is that, in fact. Our reality is embodied reality, although, like the Teacher, we can easily forget that. To help us recover wholeness, I

I used this exercise with the planning team, and they believed it was an essential part of the experience they hoped to share with the assembly. The introduction and speaking of the exercise majors in language that invites, since this type of activity is not common in worship events. We hoped to encourage people to participate to the degree they felt comfortable.

²Words and music: Dutch original by Huib Oosterhuis, tr. David Smith, harm. B. Huijbers, arr. T. Conry. Found in R. Gerald Hobbs, ed., *Songs for a Gospel People* (Winfield, B.C.: Wood Lake Books, 1987).

invite you to take part with me in an exercise of attending to the integrity of our being. The exercise will include the reading of additional verses from Ecclesiastes and will move us directly into the sermon.

I encourage you to get as physically comfortable as you can, perhaps moving out of the pew to sit or lie on the floor or just sitting with your feet flat on the floor and your arms relaxed in your lap. I suggest you close your eyes. If at any time you begin to feel uncomfortable, feel free to open your eyes or otherwise settle yourself more comfortably. Now, take a deep breath in…and breathe out. Breathe in, and release (repeated several times). Keep breathing deeply and slowly, and as you do, follow the breath through your body…to the tips of your toes…around your brain…into every nook and cranny of your being. Now follow the breath to the center of your being and rest there, letting the breath support you as it goes in…and out. It is safe there, for God is with you at your center, and you rest in the heart of God. As you rest, listen to, feel your body…Stay with your senses as I read more of the text:

I paced the exercise slowly so participants had time to "settle" in each phase.

Here we locate this basic life-reality in God, affirming God as the ultimate source of life and of all we do and as fundamentally present with us.

Scripture II: Ecclesiastes 1:1–11

Sermon: "Arguing with the Teacher"

I feel a certain kinship with the teacher. I have spent most of my life in pursuit of knowledge, and my graduate degrees must account for something. I am a professor, a teacher: I spend my days trying to help students come to new knowledge, new wisdom, a new way of living. Frankly, I find the teacher of Ecclesiastes incredibly arrogant—not unlike some of my own teachers and professors, I must admit. But I hope I am not like that. It is certainly not in the Ecclesiastical teacher's presumption of knowing the ultimate answer that I feel kinship. No, it is in despair that we are connected, despair generated by ongoing suffering in the world.

My despair deepened this summer when Amnesty International affirmed that rape and other violence toward women are running rampant across the globe. Over and over again the photographs of (name) and (name) assert the truth of that claim in our own backyard, and we know that they represent only the tip of a most gruesome and

After much group work with the scripture passage, and according to the wishes of the group, I drafted the sermon manuscript. I then returned it to the group, which engaged in constructive critique. Based on that discussion, I revised the manuscript to its present form. The group agreed that the manuscript gathered together the essentials of our discussion and served as the foundation for the whole worship event. We considered the possibility that several of us would present the sermon, but decided that singular leadership would best help coherence and flow.

We begin a series of scenarios that reflect the random, nonproductive movement of the choreography—the nongospel of the lection (tradition), the community, the cosmos. Here we named two young women, victims of gynecide, whose pictures were constantly present in the media during the trial of the man convicted of their murders.

enormous iceberg—shards of which may be shredding lives in our own homes. For twenty-five years I have been working for the valuing of women—and some of you have been doing so for far longer. We have been ridiculed, obstructed, sabotaged, and shoved aside—but the greatest abuse for us may be that gynecide, the holocaust of women, is a burgeoning global cataclysm. Jesus tried to stop it 2,000 years ago, by honoring the women he met. Vanity of vanities, says the teacher, all is vanity.

We could look elsewhere, at poverty, and its offspring, hunger and disease. One hundred thirty years ago the Salvation Army began its work of trying to eliminate these deadly plagues. But surely you have noticed the increasing number of homeless people on the streets of Toronto? We bring some of them home to us in the Out of the Cold Program—but are we really accomplishing anything? If any one gets off the street as a result, do not three or seven or fifty appear to take the vacant place? Of course Jesus said, "the poor are always with you." But he also fed the hungry by the thousands, we're told. Two thousand years later and what have we accomplished? Vanity of vanities, says the teacher, all is vanity.

Today marks the anniversary of the bombing of Hiroshima, an effort to end the war to end all wars. But the wars haven't ended. Go to any corner of the earth and you will find a war within a missile's reach. Settle one, and another erupts, full of savagery beyond our worst nightmares. "Love God, and your neighbor as yourselves," Jesus said. But day after day, thousands die for lack of love, and they are not even remembered. Vanity of vanities, says the teacher, all is vanity, an endless cycle of busyness that accomplishes nothing. There is nothing new under the sun.

But wait a minute...We do remember— Adam and Eve, Hagar and Hannah, Samson and Solomon, Dorcas and Peter, Hildegard and (name)—to name but a few. We keep birth records and set up tombstones; in Windsor and Washington the names of Viet Nam veterans are spread before the public eye. In Costa Rica, Elsa Tamez is about to build a new theological school with the names of women dead and alive inscribed probably on every surface. The prophet

With each scenario, we returned to the story of Jesus to firmly locate the roots of our experience and our hope in the One who enlivens us through all trauma, suffering, death.

Members of congregations invite homeless people into a different church each night of the week for an evening meal, conversation, games, overnight accommodation, and other amenities where available.

A third scenario attends to specific content for the day.

Here we begin to express the sudden halt of the choreography and the protest that generated it and evolved from it, ultimately evoking the gospel claim and experience. We named a woman who had been a much loved and deeply committed and involved member of the TSP congregation.

In her One Million Women project, Tamez invites women around the globe to contribute one dollar (or more, where possible) and the name of one woman per dollar they wish to

Isaiah (49:14ff, adapted) says, "Does a woman forget the baby at her breast? Or fail to cherish the child of her womb? Yet even if these forget, I will not forget you!" Even if no one else knows our name, the world is not the same for our existing our influence, our energy flow on in the cosmic symphony.

True, life is filled with recurrent cycles—winds that blow always in opposition to the turning of the earth, water that flows and evaporates and falls and flows and evaporates and falls, birth and life and death and birth and life and death. These cycles can be wearisome, they can inscribe our limitations, they can spiral us into despair. But thank God for the coming and going of rains, for the endless water-wheel without which we would either dehydrate or drown! More intimately, in the patterns, in the cadence of our very bodies, we find growth and stability. In rising and sleeping, in the rhythm of eating and drinking we find rest, nourishment, and wholeness; in the rhythm of inhale and exhale, the pulse of the heart and the circulating of our blood we discover comfort, energy, power. When our plans fail, our visions fade, and doubt and despair envelop us, in our very being in the universe we can discover ourselves at home in the heart of God. Our life itself raises up in us suspicion, resistance to the numbing, deadly claim of the teacher. The beat of our hearts proclaims a more enduring truth: God is gospel for us—God is gift of life for us, life bigger than we can comprehend no matter how many advanced degrees or how much wisdom.

The teacher's "wisdom" teaches the vanity proclaimed, because the teacher has neglected to look at the mirror of the body, refused to see the truths thumping and flowing with every beat of the heart and every breath. The teacher has refused to honor the mystery of life itself, life beyond our imagining. There is nothing new under the sun, the teacher says. Bah, humbug, we say!

Look at the face of a child and see there the wonder of a lightening bug—a tiny shining in our very own circle of dark. The bug is probably not new to us. But to the child, and in our experiencing the child—

have inscribed on the structure. The dollars help fund the construction, the inscriptions hold in visible memory the names of women who would likely otherwise be "forgotten" by the rest of the world.

We continue to move through protest and resistance to the teacher's deadly claims toward weaving together a gospel vision. Repeatedly throughout the remainder of the sermon, we describe gospel—that God is God-for-us, present with us and empowering us to engage in cocreating new life.

The centering exercise resurfaces as a means of recovering our whole-being intimacy with life-giving God.

As we worked through the text in embodied ways, we became increasingly convinced that the Ecclesiastical teacher had neglected the body and worked entirely in the head.

Here we demonstrate some of our life/death choices.

here is discovery, mystery, and newness beyond imagining! Or shall we say to the
frightened, desperate refugees of Srebrenitza
"Sorry, caring for refugees is old hat—we've
been there, done that." I dare say that the
ancient gift of a cup of cold water, for all its
antiquity, still gives them hope, promise,
power for a new tomorrow. Can we not
see in each act of kindness both the old and
the new face of God? Is it not in each writing down of a name that the ancient weaving of life is carried on anew? Like the flow
of the waters, the energy of God never
fails us.

We may waste the energy, as we often
waste water: we can spiral round and round
in our little circles like a boat with a frozen
rudder; we can spend our lives doing endless research about what we ought to do,
but never doing what we ought to do; we
can even come to TSP Sunday after Sunday for our good but never take that good
to the rest of the world—and all the while
grieve about our apparent failure to make a
difference. Then we might rightly concede
to the "wisdom" of the Ecclesiastical teacher.
But our hearts, our very breath, direct us
differently:"Take up the God-given rhythms
of creation, join together like drops of water to form a pool to wash a corner of the
world clean of corruption, gather like grains
of sand to make a whole new earth for our
exhausted global village; blend like flour,
yeast, water, and heat to make bread to feed
the hungry!"

Some of us will shape the chords un-
derlying this melody, living quietly with our
family, going back to our classroom or task
as mail carrier or job-seeker, honoring each
person we meet in her or his own right,
mirroring for the world a way apart from
violence and death-dealing. In living as lovingly as we can we act out resistance to the
teacher's despair and contribute, perhaps
with voices and notes and rhythms we cannot even hear, to the life-giving music of
the universe.

There is nothing new under the sun; all
is vanity, says the teacher. Perhaps my kinship with the teacher lies partly in arro-
gance after all. I dare—aided and abetted
by my coconspirators—to proclaim the
teacher wrong. Yes, I know the leadenness

The TSP community follows heart, breath,
beckoning of God in a variety of ways. We want
to affirm how God is already at work among
and with us, cocreating with God a reality quite
distant from the teacher's and from what much
of global existence offers.

We intentionally major in description rather
than prescription to show that we already know
many ways of participating in gospel, and that
each of us may contribute in different and often very ordinary, but equally important ways.

This section encapsulates the tension of
acceptance/resistance. We agree life is difficult, but we will not let that be the last word,
any more than God has done.

of despair in my body as well as my head. I know the weariness of slogging day after day through apparent busyness, through endless cycles that seem to get me nowhere. I know the grief of pouring my all out for the sake of others only to have my efforts ruthlessly tossed to the winds by the arrogant powerful. Who of us does not know this? But I also know that with every breath I take there is new life; with every new child, with every sunrise, with every act of compassion. I feel it in my body, in the wholeness of my being, rooted in and shaped by the very rhythms of God.

This is the wisdom of God-with-us, life-gift, for as long as we choose to exercise it. Breathe, then, with the rhythms of God's heart, and be powered into acts of resistance and new creation! Thanks be to God. Amen.

We recapitulate gospel in terms of the centering exercise and as one last impulse of empowerment and release into the activity that follows. While in print this appears as an imperative, by tone of voice and gesture it is clearly release, affirmation, invitation, encouragement.

Dipping into the Rhythm of the Waters

Located here in the font of the sanctuary and in the back are basins of water along with towels. You are invited to go to a basin, if you wish, to wash your hands clean of despair, to dabble your hands in as a reminder of the nurturing rhythms of life, and/or to remind yourself of God's love for humankind and all creation as is demonstrated in baptism. As you remain in or return to your seat, you may wish to name to yourself and to God those persons you want not to be forgotten.

"As Longs the Hart"[3]

Prayers of the People as Acts of Resistance and Empowerment

Each time we gather here, life-giving God, we act in resistance to the despair of the teacher of Ecclesiastes. We come seeking comfort, rest, and nurture in the life-rhythms of your being. Let us feel the deep healing your Spirit works; let us be suffused with dynamic power...

Each time we gather here, loving God, we refuse to forget. We come, re-membering

Now the assembly has opportunity to enact and explore in a more full-bodied way some of what they have heard or in response to what they have heard. Because all humans participate in the deep rhythms of life and in the gift of water, we opted *not* to use conventional baptismal metaphors as not all would necessarily have been baptized or recognize baptism on those terms. More, we wanted to reach behind baptism to broader experiences of water as gift, both as a way of enhancing our commitment to cherishing water and as a means of expanding common perceptions of baptism. We had no idea how many people would opt to participate in this act. Almost everyone, perhaps everyone, did and at a thoughtful pace, suggesting truly owning the moment.

The psalm setting accompanies the activity with water, emphasizing the basic human need for and hunger for water, for God. Since the water activity had the potential to be experienced as a largely private devotion even though engaged in by the assembly, the psalm began as solo, but finished as a duet as a way of embodying the move from private experience to weaving together a corporate one.

For the same reason, the prayers engage the unison voice of the assembly. They also begin to shift the focus from within the assembly toward the world. Unlike most "prayers of the people" which are often either a second

---

[3] Psalm 42. Words: Danna Harkin, Music: English folk melody. Found in *Songs for a Gospel People*.

those you have loved from generations past, named and unnamed; re-membering even those we do not know who have given themselves to the cosmic symphony, re-membering those who this day may be drowning in hopelessness or anguish:

The congregation is invited to offer aloud or in silence the names of those for whom they pray.

Each time we gather here, life-giving God, we seek newness: new wisdom, new courage, new ways of living out compassion, new notes we can add to the music of the universe…

It is because you love us that we come; we give you thanks! Amen.

Offertory Hymn: Spirit of Gentleness[4]

Offertory Prayer

Because you love us, gracious God, we bring these gifts to share,

for the sake of all in need. Amen.

Communion

The congregation is invited to gather around the table, making as large a circle as necessary to include any who wish to remain seated. The circle may be several people deep. The community is reminded that all are fully welcome, but individuals are free to participate to the degree they feel comfortable.

sermon or little more than a generic, read rehearsal of everything we ever ought pray for punctuated by repetitive responses, the prayers here come from the particular content of the service as a whole.

We opted here for the notion of remembering as *re*-membering—gathering together the members of God's global family.

This is an infrequent practice at TSP, but many present participated aloud as well, we hope, as in silence.

Congruent with moving the focus more toward our work on God's behalf in the world, the hymn affirms empowering activities of God and actively seeks continuance of them. It is the immediate basis for the offertory prayer, which the common voice of the gathering speaks.

In the meal celebration, we again invite the community to enact some of what they have heard and spoken and to experience together the communal activity of receiving and sharing God's gifts. As with the water activity, because God nurtures all and seeks all to share in nurturing others, the communion is open to everyone present. The circular gathering emphasizes the multidimensional relationality of life as opposed to those more privatized practices in which participants do not engage in receiving, eating, sharing face-to-face. Indeed, the assembly opted to disregard the invitation to gather in concentric circles, choosing instead to create a single circle.

Often "classic Eucharistic prayers" proceed as if nothing of any significance had occurred in the service up to this point. These prayers embrace core concepts of "classic eucharistic" prayers, but we constructed them intentionally out of the larger content of the service and free from the constraints of the content and structure of the presumed "norm." Given all that has gone on before, the prayers are straightforward and brief, focusing on scriptural claims about Jesus as embodier-of-gospel-par-excellence. The leadership of the prayer paragraphs rotated among three members of the planning team and the congregation.

---

[4] Words and Music: James K. Manley. Found in *Songs for a Gospel People.*

Table Prayers

When we gather at this table we remember Jesus, his acting out anew God's love for us, his habit of feeding the hungry, by the thousands or by the few.

He fed them because they were hungry, were drowning in despair, had lost their way, could not sing in the choir of the universe.

He fed them because God loved them, every one, no matter what—as God loves us, every one, no matter what.

We give thanks to you, loving God, for this table, for Jesus, who bodied forth your love, for all here and everywhere who have, in one way or another, tried to do likewise.

When we gather at this table, we feast on the promise of newness, we quench our thirst in the rhythm of life, we support one another in acts of resistance to despair, we rehearse the wisdom of compassion.

Move among us, holy One, **beginning anew in us your symphony of love, as we share gifts of life with one another, and with our ever needy world.**

(The presider breaks, pours, starts elements around with the invitation to feast on the bread of promise and quench thirst in the rhythm of life. Elements are offered to any who did not come to the table.)

Not only do we affirm and celebrate God-for-us, we also name and seek empowerment for our responsibility of embodying gospel among those most in need.

We did not include an interpretive narrative ("verba" or "institution narrative") for a variety of reasons. Included among these is the hermeneutical and theological issue of privileging these quite varied biblical texts. In our view, perhaps attested to by the very name many communities choose to call this event, "communion" occurs not by pronouncing a set of words as warrant or act of consecration, but in the act of thankfully sharing God's loving, nourishing gifts with others.[5] The whole service points to this, and the activity of the table concretely embodies it. The community is responsible for seeing that each other has enough to eat/drink. This models their responsibility to so embody gospel in the rest of life.

As the meal is an event of the whole, so also the prayer belongs to the whole, and further enhances the progress of moving this gospel experience out into the streets and highways of the world.

As is my habit when presiding, I constructed the blessing out of the content of the service *as event* and consequently gave it extemporaneously. I am unable to reconstruct it here.

This song affirms our engagement in the collaborative process of new creation. The congregation is invited to move with the music so they can do what they are singing.

We wanted to keep the momentum of the communal circle going. We planned that while the people were still in the circle, at the start of the last verse, I (as the official presider) would turn to team members on my right and left, greet them with peace, and then exit down the central aisle. The team members would replicate my actions, thereby initiating the process all around the circle. There was no postlude as the song was to serve as a recessional for the entire assembly. However, the community had decided after the postmeal prayer to return to the pews. The planning team still followed the plan, each initiating the action in the pews here and there along the way. The congregation followed in kind.

---

[5] The literature addressing the provenance, interpretation, and appropriate use of these words is vast and can hardly be reviewed here. Of particular interest to me in this regard is Mack, *A Myth of Innocence.*

Post-meal Prayer:
Loved, nurtured, enlivened by you,
God of wholeness, help us live our
thanks lending our voices, our hearts,
ourselves to create with you the music
of the universe. Amen.

Blessing

Hymn: Turning of the World[6]
The congregation is invited to go out
to play and work during the singing of the
last verse.

After the event, the team listened to comments of participants and then gathered to discuss what we had accomplished. Responses from the community confirmed that we had effectively followed our map and achieved our goal, and that the congregation had found this to be an event of gospel, life-giving and enabling of living faithfully in a complex world.

This script presents but one effort at collaborative, constructive worship. It does not pretend to be perfect or definitive, nor to embrace everything that we might imagine good worship ought to do over time. At the same time, this event is but one of many in which I or some of my students have used the same process, and although I have yet to design a really thorough process for assessing the effectiveness of the work, each experience strengthens my conviction of the viability of the design. Evaluating such experiences does present significant challenges, since not everything can be assessed in immediacy. It may be years or generations before a particular gospel moment bears fruit, or shows itself to be death dealing—so limited, Calvin would say, is human "vision." Yet criteria for assessment are implicit in the design. They include letting fully embodied love of God for us and us for God, self and others be the ground and the guide—marked by such features as openness and flexibility, honoring diversity, partnering and interrelationality, attending to the wholeness of being, a hermeneutic of dynamism and of suspicion, of imagination and vision.

To some this approach may seem revolutionary or sheer folly. Gospel, it seems to me, can be similarly described. Those who choose to participate actively in gospel have to trust God to be fully invested in the wholeness of reality and in each person on earth. We also have to learn to take delight in surprises instead of being certain about what comes next, to give up on notions of control and perfection and instead value authenticity and sometimes bare-boned honesty and even failure. Yet if we believe in incarnation, then surely we know that God works with us as we learn new ways of living in loving, dialogical relationship with God and all God's beloved family of friends.

---

[6] Folk song by Ruth Pelham, source unknown.

PART VI

Coming Full Circle

CHAPTER 16

Life as Worship

Our reality is the interplay of ecosystems. We do not live as independent entities. Even though our embodiment seems to be largely self-contained, we constantly interact with our environment. We breathe in and exhale. We ingest foods and liquids that grow out of the earth or come from our coinhabitants on this planet, coinhabitants who are themselves largely dependent on the fruit of the earth for their existence. We release into the environment gasses, fluids, and solids we cannot use. We use global energies—gravity, air currents, tides, fossil fuels—to get where we are going and to do and make what we want.

We also expend our energies *into* the ecosystem: digging and hoeing the earth to help it grow bigger and better, hacking away at icebergs to free trapped whales, exhausting ourselves fighting lightning-ignited forest fires. On the other hand, we also turn prime farmlands into subdivisions and landfills, pour endless streams of vicious chemicals into streams, and bury toxic wastes in the soil. We rip up ancient forests to feed the relentlessly gaping maw of consumerism, and reap a harvest of unbreathable air, undrinkable water, inedible food, intolerable sun...

Toronto is only one of several North American metropolitan cities of my acquaintance. It is still livable, at least for people of some means. But cities everywhere are growing by leaps and bounds, and many people who live in these crowded, noisy, polluted places, who eat plastic food and drink God-knows-what chemicals, find it hard *not* to become selfish, aggressive, miserable, dehumanized consumers of everything they can get their hands on by whatever means, even violence. Give us a chance to make a decent living where we can breathe fresh air, enjoy quiet, have a bit of elbow room and natural beauty, give us a second chance at clean

167

water and food, and there is a possibility we will begin to live differently. We may plant new trees, preserve parklands, fight to keep elephants and dolphins from extinction; create green jobs for the unemployed, and become builders of healthy relationships with our ecosystems. The way we function effects the ecosystem in which we live, and the ecosystem effects us, like it or not.

We see the same thing in families. If you grow up in a family that abuses its children or is chemically dependent, chances are pretty good that you, too, will become a child abuser or a drug user. If, on the other hand, you grow up knowing yourself loved just because you exist, chances are pretty good you will have a healthy self-image and be accepting of others. If at home you are praised for your talents but at school are mocked by classmates and get poor grades, you may grow up confused, sometimes thinking you are an absolute worm, other times thinking you are the best thing since the worldwide web.

You will probably think and feel the wrong way at the worst possible time—useless and incompetent at the critical job interview, stunningly brilliant when you are washing your dog. Naturally, the search committee will pick up on your self-perception of the moment, and so may your dog, for better or worse. You may ruin the chairperson's day, and she may go home and snap at her kids on account of you. The kids may bully the neighbor kid who will disobey his parents who will vote against the creative idea of converting human waste and trash into fuel and for the dangerous ones of continuing to pour raw sewage into the ocean and plowing trash into landfills, just because they don't feel like fighting the tide… Meanwhile your overly-affectionate pet will be slobbering unrestrainedly over someone who is deathly allergic to animals. But it is not really a humorous matter. We live in interrelating ecosystems, shaping them and being shaped by them, like it or not, toward life or toward death.

God for Us, Us for God

The fact that we have experienced the grace of God in Christ Jesus, that we are invited to live in loving, dialogical relationship with God and neighbor, looms large here. But let us try to see this once more from the ground up. God expresses the divine self *for us*, beckoning us into loving relationship. Perhaps we experience this most internally. Augustine and Calvin described it as a restlessness of the heart that never settles until the heart finds God. Perhaps this conscious encounter arises out of one of the external ecosystems in which we exist: a deadly one from which we seek escape and that drives us into God's arms; or a lively one that makes us feel like we have always belonged and that embodies the life to which we can finally say, YES! In any case, the experience of God-for-us and us-for-God, this event of the divine and human ecosystems interrelating in a new way for us, becomes an event of worship.

Worship events are particular occasions of God giving the divine self to us. They are also moments of our bringing to God who and what we are. The ecosphere of God and our human sphere come together in purposeful, life-giving conjunction. We are overwhelmed by God's astonishing love, awed by divine splendor. We are shamed to tears and anguish by divine justice, forgiven into laughter and love by divine graciousness.

Meanwhile, do we think God remains immutable, unaffected, unmoved by us? Not so. God is with us in all our reality, eating and drinking with us, walking and talking with us, suffering with us through the worst kind of betrayal and death, rejoicing and laughing with us in the gift of life...God *is* affected by us—frustrated by our stubbornness, grieved to death by our betrayal, brought to tears by our pleas for help. Our Compassionate Companion moves heaven and earth to be for us what we most need God to be, *with* us.

Mediated in Community

Private experiences of intimacy with God are an important dimension of this life-giving relationship. Yet ultimately, encounter with God leads to a reconfiguring of ecosystems, often including a new connection, or a new kind of connection with a specific community, a particular gathering of Christians. Like every individual, a congregation is also a minisystem within the great sphere of God. Like all ecosystems, it both gives to us and receives from us. Through the thoughts, mouths, hands, eyes of others, we receive the gifts of God for us. So also we convey them by a hug and the wink of an eye, in caring conversation and putting our money in the offering plate. Meanwhile, the *way* those gifts are expressed, as well as the gifts themselves, shapes our reality, our individual ecosystem, and the ecosystem of the whole community.

Changes

No community is ever quite the same once we have been in its midst, nor are we the same. In fact, none of our interrelating spheres is ever the same once we affirm life-giving connection with the divine ecology. We live differently, individually and communally, when we opt to accept God's invitation. When we choose to interact positively in the divine ecosystem, we begin to see all our interrelating ecosystems in a new light. We claim our bodies not just as personal containers and conveyances and our minds not just as data processors, but the wholeness of our being as the home of

God's Spirit. We use our church buildings not as sacred space to be protected from profanation by the secular world, but as a gift to be put to use as a resource and life-source for God's global family.

We live in the world not as coincidental framework, but as the locus of God's being with us and our being with others. We live with family not only as those with whom we have blood and genetic ties, nor even as those with whom we have baptismal ties, but as those with whom we are sisters and brothers on account of incarnation. We take responsibility for authentic, caring, constructive interaction with all our arenas of being, because anything else is antithetical to relationship with God who is the source of life. So, worship consists of more than private devotions, more than what happens when Christians gather for sermon and hymn and prayer. Worship is life lived out in loving, dialogical relationship with God and God's global family. Worship is participating graciously in God's multi-relational ecosystem.

On the Large Scale

The interrelationship between individual and communal ecosystems within the ecclesial family of God also persists between the congregation and the community which is its context, whether it be neighborhood or village. The way in which the congregation relates to that larger community shapes the community, and the way the community relates to the congregation shapes the congregation. We do not, either as individual or as congregation, function independently of the corner of State and Michigan, the Centers for Disease Control, the Don Jail—or whatever landmarks and events are the context of our particular congregation. What goes on in those places is part of our reality, as individuals and as a congregation of the whole.

This means that the premise of the separation of church and state, sacred and secular is nothing short of fraudulent. Secular, civic, provincial, national, global issues belong in the worship life of the church, in the same way our personal struggles do.

So we pray for persons who are sick and governments that are diseased, we pray for pastors and presidents, we pray for justice and peace for aboriginal peoples around the globe, for the restoration of rain forest and ozone layer. But it isn't enough to pray, though surely God is affected and thus change can occur. It isn't enough to pray, because we in fact are God's bodies in this world. So we send out medical missionaries and teachers, provide sanctuary for political refugees and homeless folk, write editorials and denominational position papers on social justice issues, reconfigure our lifestyles to reduce, reuse, recycle.

How much more worshipful will our life in interrelated ecosystems be when our worship events themselves become more intentionally and intensely relational, when we find time and place and manner for being present *for each other* as fully as God is present for us? How much more empowering will our life in interrelated ecosystems be when we shape our worship events dialogically, when we speak and sing together face-to-face and eye-to-eye—not just pastor and people, but all of us? How much more gospel-laden will our lives be when members of all ages and abilities take part in constructing sermon and the rest of worship content so that all participants experience living in interdependent ecosystems, with each sharing responsibility for the life of the whole, so that every participant is practiced in the process of reshaping ecosystems by love and grace? How much more just will our life in interrelated ecosystems be when we intentionally engage in exploring the life-issues of our global village with regard to God's dream and work for us and what we can do to constructively impact that whole; when we vigorously confess not just our belief in God but *that* our belief in God is commitment to the life and health of God's whole creation? How much more life-giving will our life-in-interrelated ecosystems be when instead of telling our congregation each Sunday to go and serve God, we as a congregation expand into the world the shared act of relationship we have built together in planning and implementing this day's worship event?

For the Life of the Cosmos

What we do in worship events shapes us and the entire world in which we live—intentionally or unintentionally. If our worship events essentially serve to keep safely enclosed a closet congregation, then we are unfaithful to the gospel that calls us to love our neighbors as ourselves, and we are contributing to the death not only of ourselves, but of every sphere with which we interrelate. We finally have no one to blame but ourselves if acid rains keep falling and fish stocks continue to vanish and the weather grows ever more bizarre as a result of global warming. On the other hand, if our worship events serve to enliven us and support us in our ecological interrelationships, then we begin to be, as Luther suggested, not only Christ for each other, but for our desperately needy world.

We cannot be Christians in isolation. Take us out of our community of support, the ecosystem that intends to enable our encounter with the One Who Gives Life, and our resources for living in the face of death diminish with incredible speed. So the worship life of the community needs to be an incredible source of strength—but it also needs to be *fully present in the cosmos of interrelating ecosystems it inhabits.*

Incarnation = Interdependence

Thus the Eastern liturgical theology is, to my mind, only half right. Worship events there are understood as taking us out of this world and lifting us up into heaven.

But if heaven then does not accompany us into our reality, we are truly lost. For this *is* our reality: this street, this neighborhood, this town or city, this province, this nation, this continent, this world, this universe. It is where we live and if God is not present with us in all our interrelationships with our reality, in all our interrelating and interdependent ecosystems then we have misunderstood incarnation altogether.

So our worship will reflect our being in the world. It will envision it in new ways, it will empower our being in our global ecology, it will embody dialogue with all our realities quite beyond the 12 o'clock hour and the sanctuary doors. Faithfulness to gospel is more than preaching a stirring sermon, more than reciting the correct words, more than doing the rite right. It is engaging all our interrelated ecosystems in loving, dialogical relationship with God, or else it is death.

We belong with God, we belong with one another, and we belong with the world. What we do with that is what we do in our worship events, for they are primordial means of manifesting relationship between us and God and all God's creation—and they are fundamental shapers of all our interrelating ecosystems, for better or worse. So we need to be intentional about worship events being microcosmic experiences of interrelationship between the divine and human ecosystems. We need to be intentional about shaping worship events so that they affirm our interdependence with and our responsibility for all our interrelating spheres. How will this worship element, this worship event, directly affect all our ecosystems? In what way will this hymn, prayer, sermon, or order of worship directly work to reconfigure our interrelating spheres in terms of God's gracious love? What will this worship event do to enable us to body forth gospel, to enliven this earth, this whole earth, to the glory of God?

Afterword

Those of you who have stuck with me to the end now recognize, if you did not before, that there are many possible responses to the questions we've asked and issues we've raised. Indeed, we might and probably should ask many more questions and raise many more issues. And unlike the choice between the two paths diverging in Frost's yellow wood,[1] we can map many possible processes for worshiping faithfully.

As our world changes at faster than light speed, though, and we find it harder and harder to keep up with our disciplines, our employer's demands, our children, and all the necessities of our lives, we may be tempted to pull our heads into our stained-glass shells and seek sanctuary under the roof of worship tradition. Alternately, we may be tempted to pull the quilt up over our heads and forget Sunday morning altogether. If so, I hope this book—with the help of the ever-moving Spirit—will beckon us and tug at us to keep moving, too, to recognize that the work of exploring worship and of creating worshiping anew needs to go on as long as people are dying for want of gospel.

What happens after the final point of punctuation of this book depends on all of us. Each of us is responsible in some way for working with God at constructing worship events that empower us to engage in the work of giving life to the world. Were will you begin? What worship habit will you pick up and probe for its current value? What idea, dream, or vision will you try on for size? Whom might you ask to be your co-workers in this enterprise of going perhaps where no one has gone before?

Where to begin? Perhaps with deep breathing, with once again renewing our awareness that the life within us is gift, gift to share. Where to begin? Perhaps with deep breathing, and the sure and certain knowledge buried deep within our DNA and carried with every drop of blood and in every breath we take that we are God's bodies, and that the one who guides our worshiping journey is the Source, the Incarnation, and the Power of Love.

Let it be so.

---

[1] "Two roads diverged in a yellow wood, and sorry I could not travel both and be one traveler, long I stood…" "The Road Not Taken," *The Mentor Book of American Poets*, 250.

Bibliography

Abbott, W., ed. *Documents of Vatican II.* Grand Rapids: Eerdmans, 1975.

Adams, Carol J. and Marie M. Fortune, eds. *Violence Against Women and Children: A Christian Theological Sourcebook.* New York: Continuum, 1995.

Adams, Doug. *Congregational Dancing in Christian Worship.* Austin: The Sharing Company, 1971.

Augustine. "de Trinitate," 12,7,10 in *Nicene and Post-Nicene Fathers,* vol. 3. Grand Rapids: Eerdmans, 1956.

Augustine. "On Christian Doctrine," in *A Select Library of the Nicene and Post-Nicene Fathers of the Christian Church,* vol. 2. Philip Schaff, ed. Edinburgh: T&T Clark/Grand Rapids: Eerdmans: 1890/1993, I (36) 40.

Augustine. "Our Lord's Sermon on the Mount," *The Preaching of Augustine,* J. Pelikan, ed. Francine Cardman, tr. Philadelphia: Fortress Press, 1973.

Augustine. "Sermon 229," *Fathers of the Church,* vol. 38. Sister Mary Muldowney, R.S.M. New York: Fathers of the Church, 1959.

Augustine. "Tractate on John," in *A Select Library of the Nicene and Post-Nicene Fathers of the Christian Church,* vol. 7. Philip Schaff, ed. Trans. John Gibb and James Innes, Edinburgh: T. & T. Clark/Grand Rapids: Eerdmans: 1890/1993.

Barth, Karl. *Prayer.* Don E. Saliers, ed. Sara F. Terrien, tr. Philadelphia: Westminster Press, 1985.

Benedict, Daniel and Craig Kennet Miller. *Contemporary Worship for the 21st Century: Worship or Evangelism?* Nashville: Discipleship Resources, 1994.

Black, Kathy. *A Healing Homiletic: Preaching and Disability.* Nashville: Abingdon Press, 1996.

Bouley, Allan. *From Freedom to Formula.* Washington: Catholic University of America Press, 1981.

Bradshaw, Paul F. *The Search for the Origins of Christian Worship: Sources & Methods for the Study of Early Liturgy.* New York: Oxford University Press, 1992.

Brown, Joanne Carlson, and Carole R. Bohn, eds. *Christianity, Patriarchy and Abuse.* New York: Pilgrim Press, 1989.

Brueggemann, Walter. *Finally Comes the Poet: Daring Speech for Proclamation.* Minneapolis: Fortress Press, 1989.

Burghardt, Walter B., S.J. *Preaching, The Art and The Craft.* New York: Paulist Press, 1987.

Burkhart, John E. *Worship: A Searching Examination of the Liturgical Experience*. Philadelphia: Westminster Press, 1982.

Buttrick, David. *Homiletic: Moves and Structures*. Philadelphia: Fortress Press, 1987.

Calvin, John. *Institutes of the Christian Religion*. John T. McNeill, ed. F. L. Battles, tr. (from the 1559 Latin Text edited by Barth and Neisel, [*Joannis Calvini Opera Selecta* Vol. 3, 4,5] including collations from earlier editions of that text and versions of the Institutes). Philadelphia: Westminster Press, 1960.

Caron, Charlotte. *To Make and Make Again: Feminist Ritual Thealogy*. New York: Crossroad, 1993.

Chupungco, Anscar J. *Liturgical Inculturation: Sacramentals, Religiosity, and Catechesis*. Collegeville, Minnesota: Liturgical Press, 1992.

Chupungco, Anscar J., OSB. *Liturgies of the Future: The Process and Methods of Inculturation*. New York: Paulist Press, 1989.

Costen, Melva Wilson. *African American Christian Worship*. Nashville: Abingdon Press, 1993.

Craddock, Fred B. *As One Without Authority*. Enid: Phillips University Press, 1974.

Craddock, Fred B. *Preaching*. Nashville: Abingdon Press, 1985.

Crawford, Evans E. and Thomas H. Troeger. *The Hum: Call and Response in African American Preaching*. Nashville: Abingdon Press, 1995.

Cuming, G. J., ed., *Hippolytus: A Text for Students*. Bramcote Notts: Grove Press, 1976.

Cyprian. "The Epistles of Cyprian: To Cæcilius, on the Sacrament of the Cup of the Lord." *The Ante-Nicene Fathers*. Alexander Roberts and James Donaldson, eds. Edinburgh: T&T Clark/ Grand Rapids: Eerdmans, 1990.

Damascene, St. John, "Concerning the Holy Icons," in Constantine Cavarnos, *The Icon: Its Spiritual Basis and Purpose*. Haverhill, Massachusetts: Institute for Byzantine and Modern Greek Studies, 1973.

Dawn, Marva J. *Reaching Out without Dumbing Down: A Theology of Worship for the Turn-of-the-Century Culture*. Grand Rapids: Eerdmans, 1995.

Driver, Tom F. *The Magic of Ritual: Our Need for Liberating Rites that Transform Our Lives and Our Communities*. San Francisco: Harper, 1991.

Doran, Carol and Thomas H. Troeger. *Trouble at the Table: Gathering the Tribes for Worship*. Nashville: Abingdon Press, 1992.

Elkins, Heather Murray. *Worshiping Women: Reforming God's People for Praise*. Nashville: Abingdon Press, 1994.

Ecumenism. "The Many Shapes of Sacred Space." September, 1996.

Environment and Art in Catholic Worship. Washington: National Conference of Catholic Bishops, 1978.

Farris, Stephen. "Reformed Identity and Reformed Worship." *Reformed World* (June 1993).

Farris, Stephen. "The New Testament, the Holy and Reformed Identity." *Encounter* 57/4 (Autumn 1996).

Frost, Robert. "Mending Wall," and "The Road Not Taken," Williams, Oscar and Edwin Honig, eds. *The Mentor Book of Major American Poets*. New York and Scarborough, Ontario: The New American Library, 1962.

Fuller, Reginald H. *What is Liturgical Preaching?* London: SCM Press, 1957.

Gelineau, J., S.J. "Music and Singing in the Liturgy." *The Study of Liturgy*, rev. ed. Cheslyn Jones, Geoffrey Wainwright, Edward Yarnold, S.J., Paul Bradshaw, eds. London: SPCK, 1992.

Hilkert, Mary Catherine. *Naming Grace: Preaching and the Sacramental Imagination*. New York: Continuum, 1997.

Hobbs, R. Gerald. *Songs for a Gospel People*. Winfield, B.C.: Wood Lake Books, 1987.

Hodgson, Peter C. *Winds of the Spirit: A Constructive Christian Theology*. Louisville: Westminster/John Knox Press, 1994.

Hoon, Paul. *The Integrity of Worship*. Nashville: Abingdon Press, 1971.

Hopewell, James F. *Congregation: Stories and Structure*. Philadelphia: Fortress Press, 1987.

Hunter, David G., ed. *Marriage in the Early Church*. Minneapolis: Augsburg/Fortress Press, 1992.

Irwin, Kevin J. *Context and Text: Method in Liturgical Theology*. Collegeville, Minn.: Pueblo, 1994.

Johnson, Elizabeth A. *Consider Jesus: Waves of Renewal in Christology*. New York: Crossroad, 1990.

Johnson, Elizabeth A. *She Who Is: The Mystery of God in Feminist Theological Discourse*. New York: Crossroad, 1992.

Justin. "First Apology," *Early Christian Fathers, Vol. I*, chap. 65, 67. *Library of Christian Classics,* Cyril C. Richardson, ed. Philadelphia: Westminster Press, 1953.

Kalokyris, Constantine. "The Content of Eastern Iconography." *Concilium* 132.

Keir, Thomas H. *The Word in Worship: Preaching and its Setting in Common Worship.* London: Oxford University Press, 1962.

Lathrop, Gordon W. *Holy Things: A Liturgical Theology.* Minneapolis: Fortress Press, 1993.

Long, Thomas G. *The Witness of Preaching.* Louisville: Westminster/John Knox Press, 1989.

Lowry, Eugene L. *Living with the Lectionary: Preaching Through the Revised Common Lectionary.* Nashville: Abingdon Press, 1992.

Lowry, Eugene L. *The Sermon: Dancing the Edge of Mystery.* Nashville: Abingdon Press, 1997.

Luther, Martin. "The Adoration of the Sacrament." *LW 36.* Philadelphia: Muhlenberg Press, 1959.

Luther, Martin. "Against the Fanatics." *LW 36.*

Luther, Martin. "The Large Catechism." *The Book of Concord: The Confessions of the Evangelical Lutheran Church.* Theodore G. Tappert, Tr., ed. Philadelphia: Fortress Press, 1959.

Luther, Martin. "Sermon for the Early Christmas Service." *LW* 52.

Luther, Martin. "Sermon on the Mount." *LW* 21, St. Louis: Concordia, 1954.

Mack, Burton L. *A Myth of Innocence: Mark and Christian Origins.* Minneapolis: Fortress Press, 1988.

Maldonado, Luis. "Art in the Liturgy." *Symbol and Art in Worship.* Concilium 132, David N. Power and Luis Maldonado, eds. 1980.

McClure, John S. *The Four Codes of Preaching: Rhetorical Strategies* Minneapolis: Fortress Press, 1991.

McClure, John S. *The Round-Table Pulpit: Where Leadership and Preaching Meet.* Nashville: Abingdon Press, 1995.

McFague, Sallie. *The Body of God: An Ecological Theology.* Minneapolis: Fortress Press, 1993.

McFague, Sallie. *Metaphorical Theology.* Philadelphia: Fortress Press, 1982.

McKenna, John H. "Infant Baptism: Theological Reflections." *Worship* 70/1 (May 1996).

Melloh, John Allyn, SM and William G. Storey, eds. *Praise God in Song: Ecumenical Daily Prayer.* Chicago: GIA Publications, Inc., 1979.

Mitchell, Henry H. *Black Preaching: The Recovery of a Powerful Art.* Nashville: Abingdon Press, 1990.

Mitchell, Nathan. "The Amen Corner." *Worship* 67/1 (January 1993).

Mitchell, Nathan, "The Dissolution of the Rite of Christian Initiation." *Made, not Born: New Perspectives on Christian Initiation and the*

Catechumenate. Notre Dame: University of Notre Dame Press, 1976.

Moeller, Pamela Ann. *A Kinesthetic Homiletic: Embodying Gospel in Preaching*. Minneapolis: Fortress Press, 1993.

Moeller, Pamela Ann. *Calvin's Doxology: Worship in the 1559 Institutes with a View to Contemporary Worship Renewal*. Allison Park, Penn.: Pickwick Publications, 1997.

Moeller, Pamela Ann. "Worship as Hermeneutic: Interpreter of the Gospel." *Consensus* 16/1 (1990): 27–44.

Pfatteicher, Philip H. *Commentary on the Lutheran Book of Worship*. Minneapolis: Augsburg Fortress, 1990.

Power, David N. *Unsearchable Riches: The Symbolic Nature of Liturgy*. New York: Pueblo, 1984.

Power, David N. *Worship: Culture & Theology*. Washington: Pastoral Press, 1990.

Procter-Smith, Marjorie. *In Her Own Rite: Constructing Feminist Liturgical Tradition*. Nashville: Abingdon Press, 1990.

Procter-Smith, Marjorie. *Praying With Our Eyes Open: Engendering Feminist Liturgical Prayer*. Nashville: Abingdon Press, 1995.

Reid, Robert, Jeffrey Bullock and David Fleer. "Preaching as the Creation of Experience: The Not-So-Rational Revolution of the New Homiletic." *The Journal of Communication and Religion* 18/1 (1995).

Rice, Charles L. *The Embodied Word: Preaching as Art & Liturgy*. Minneapolis: Fortress, 1991.

Rock, Judith, and Norman Mealy. *Performer as Priest & Prophet*. San Francisco: Harper & Row, 1988.

Rock, Judith. *Theology in the Shape of Dance: Using Dance and Worship in Theological Process*. Austin: The Sharing Company, 1978.

Roll, Susan K. "Beyond Dualistic Models of Festal Time," presented at the Congress "Lichamelijkheid, Religie en Gender," Fontana Nieuweschans Landelijk Onderzoeksprogramma, Nederland, December, 1997.

Rose, Lucy Atkinson. *Sharing the Word: Preaching in the Roundtable Church*. Louisville: Westminster John Knox, 1997.

Ruether, Rosemary Radford. *Women-Church*. San Francisco: Harper and Row, 1986.

Saliers, Don E. "Prayer and Emotion: Shaping and Expressing Christian Life." *Christians at Prayer*, John Gallen, S.J., ed. Notre Dame: University of Notre Dame Press, 1977.

Saliers, Don E. *Worship as Theology: Foretaste of Glory Divine*. Nashville: Abingdon Press, 1994.

Schmemann, Alexander. *For the Life of the World: Sacraments and Orthodoxy*. Crestwood, New York: St. Vladimir's Seminary Press, 1973.

Service Book for the Use of Ministers Conducting Public Worship. The United Church of Canada, 1969.

Skudlarek, William. *The Word in Worship: Preaching in a Liturgical Context*. Nashville: Abingdon Press, 1981.

Smart, David Howard. *Primitive Christians: Baroque Architecture and Worship in Restoration London*, Th.D. diss., 1997.

Stookey, Laurence Hull. *Baptism: Christ's Act in the Church*. Nashville: Abingdon Press, 1982.

Stookey, Laurence Hull. *Eucharist: Christ's Feast with the Church*. Nashville: Abingdon Press, 1993.

Suchocki, Marjorie Hewitt. *In God's Presence: Theological Reflections on Prayer*. St. Louis: Chalice Press, 1996.

Taussig, Hal. *The Lady of the Dance*. Austin: The Sharing Company, 1981.

Taussig, Hal. *New Categories for Dancing the Old Testament*. Austin: The Sharing Company, 1981.

Taylor, Margaret. "A History of Symbolic Movement in Worship," in *Dance as Religious Studies*. Adams, Doug & Diane Apostolos-Cappadona, eds. New York: Crossroad, 1990.

Samuel Terrien. *The Elusive Presence: The Heart of Biblical Theology*. San Francisco: Harper & Row, 1978.

Tertullian. "On the Apparel of Women." 1,1, in *Ante-Nicene Fathers*, Vol. 4. Grand Rapids: Eerdmans, 1965.

Troeger, Thomas H. "Emerging New Standards in the Evaluation of Effective Preaching," *Worship* 64/4 (1990).

Tubbs Tisdale, Leonora. *Preaching as Local Theology and Folk Art*. Minneapolis: Fortress Press, 1997.

Uzukwu, Elochukwu E. *Worship as Body Language: Introduction to Christian Worship: An African Orientation*. Collegeville, Minnesota: Liturgical Press, 1997.

Van Seters, Arthur. *Preaching as a Social Act: Theology and Practice*. Nashville: Abingdon Press, 1988.

Van Seters, Arthur. "Preaching as an Oral/Aural Act." Papers of the Annual Meeting of the Academy of Homiletics, 1989.

Vogel, Cyrille. "Symbols in Christian Worship: Food and Drink." *Concilium* 132.

Voices United: The Hymn and Worship Book of the United Church of Canada. Toronto: United Church Publishing House, 1996.

Walton, Janet R. *Art and Worship: A Vital Connection.* Wilmington, Delaware: Michael Glazier, 1988.

Wainwright, Geoffrey. *Doxology: The Praise of God in Worship, Doctrine, and Life; A Systematic Theology.* New York: Oxford University Press, 1980.

Ware, Ann Patrick. "The Easter Vigil: A Theological and Liturgical Critique." In *Women at Worship: Interpretations of North American Diversity.* eds. Marjorie Procter-Smith and Janet R. Walton, Louisville: Westminster/John Knox Press, 1993.

Weber, Joanna. "The Sacred in Art: Introducing Father Marie-Alain Couturier's Aesthetic," *Worship* 69/3 (May 1995): 243–262.

Webster's Ninth Collegiate Dictionary. Springfield, Massachusetts: Merriam-Webster.

White, James F. *A Brief History of Christian Worship.* Nashville: Abingdon Press, 1993.

White, James F. *Sacraments as God's Self Giving.* Nashville: Abingdon Press, 1983.

White, James F. *Introduction to Christian Worship.* Nashville: Abingdon Press, 1981.

White, James F. "The Words of Worship." *Christian Century* (December 13, 1978).

Willimon, William. *Preaching and Leading Worship.* Philadelphia: Westminster, 1984.

Wilson, Paul S. *Imagination of the Heart: New Understandings in Preaching.* Nashville: Abingdon Press, 1988.

Wilson, Paul S. "Paul's Letters: A Homiletical Perspective." *Toronto Journal of Theology* 11/1 (Spring 1995).

Wilson, Paul S. *The Practice of Preaching.* Nashville: Abingdon Press, 1995.

Yarnold, Edward, S.J. *The Awe Inspiring Rites of Initiation: Baptismal Homilies of the Fourth Century.* Slough, England: St. Paul Publications, 1971.